THE GREAT
BOOK OF ALASKA

The Crazy History of Alaska with
Amazing Random Facts & Trivia

**A Trivia Nerds Guide
to the History of the
United States Vol.5**

BILL O'NEILL

DON'T FORGET YOUR FREE BOOKS

CONTENTS

CHAPTER FOUR

INTRODUCTION

How much do you know about the state of Alaska?

Sure, you know Alaska is a cold state that's dark for most of the year. You know it's snow-covered for most of the year and that it's a popular place for nature lovers to visit. But what else do you *really* know about Alaska?

Do you know which country owned Alaska first?

Have you ever wondered how Alaska got its name or its state nickname "The Last Frontier"?

You know the state is home to grizzly bears and polar bears, but have you heard of the many Inuit legendary creatures that are said to haunt the state? Do you know about the serial killer that once murdered women in Alaska?

You've heard about the Alaskan natives, but how much do you really know about their culture and customs? What do you know about modern-day Alaskan natives?

If you have ever wondered about the answers to any of these questions, you've come to the right place. This book is full of stories and facts about the state of Alaska.

This isn't just any book about Alaska. It will highlight some of the key facts that have helped shape Alaska into the state it is today. You'll learn answers to some of the things you may have wondered about the state, as well as facts about the state that you've never even wondered about. Once you've finished reading, you'll know everything there is to know about Alaska.

Alaska is a state that's rich in both history and culture. We'll go back in time before Alaska became a part of the United States. We'll jump around as we take a look at some of the most interesting facts about the state's history.

While we will stick mostly to a timeline of historical events, we'll also jump around as we take a look at Alaska's historic past. We'll also talk about the state's pop culture, sports, and more.

This book is broken up into easy to follow chapters that will help you learn more about the Last Frontier. Once you have finished each chapter, you can also test your knowledge with trivia questions.

Some of the facts you'll read about in this book will be sad. Some of them will be shocking. Some of them will creep you out. But the one thing all of these facts have in common is that they're all fascinating!

Once you've finished reading this book, you're guaranteed to walk away with a wealth of knowledge about Alaska.

This book will answer the following questions:

Where did Alaska get its state nickname?

Which famous animal hero came from the state?

What movie, which was based on a true story, was filmed in the state?

What classic American novel was inspired by Alaska's Klondike Gold Rush?

Which Alaskan musician's family has a reality TV show about life in the state?

What serial killer came out of Alaska?

What monster is believed to be lurking in Iliamna Lake?

And so much more!

CHAPTER ONE

ALASKA'S HISTORY AND \RANDOM FACTS

Alaska became the 49th state to join the Union in 1959. Have you ever wondered how the state got its name or what country the territory belonged to before it became a part of the U.S.? Do you know why Alaska is known as the Last Frontier? Do you know which famous American hero came from the state? Read on to find out these and other facts about the state of Alaska!

Alaska Has Been a State for Less Than 100 Years

You probably already know that Alaska was the second to last state to join the United States, but did you know that it hasn't been a state for a very long time at all? In fact, Alaska is less than 100 years old!

In 1959, the proclamation admitting Alaska as a U.S. state was signed by President Dwight Eisenhower. The 49-star American flag was also released at that time.

Hawaii became a state the very same year, which eventually led to the release of the 50-star American flag.

The United States Bought Alaska From Another Country

Did you know the United States bought the state of Alaska from another country? Do you know which country that is? Russia!

Russia's ownership of the area that is now known as Alaska dates back to the 1700s. In 1741, a Dane by the name of Vitus Bering led a Russian expedition to the region. When they arrived, they found a lot of animals in the region. This meant wealth because animal furs were very valuable.

By 1772, the Russians had settled in Unalaska. In 1978, they also settled on Kodiak Island.

By the 1860s, however, Russia no longer saw the benefit in Alaska. The fur supply had begun to diminish due to overhunting, and they also found it difficult to supply their bases from such a long distance. Due to their lack of interest, they decided to try to sell Alaska to the United States.

In 1867, William Seward, who was then U.S. Secretary of State under President Andrew Jackson's administration, bought the territory. He paid two cents per acre or $7.2 million for the 586,000 square miles. The transaction is formally known in history as "The Alaska Purchase."

At the time, the purchase was highly controversial, with many believing it was a pointless purchase. The press even ridiculed the decision. It was referred to as "Seward's folly," "Seward's icebox," and "President Jackson's polar bear garden."

When Seward first purchased the land, the area was first recognized as the Department of Alaska. In 1884, it became known as the District of Alaska. Then it later went on to become a state in 1959.

The Meaning of the Name "Alaska"

Have you ever wondered where the name "Alaska" came from?

The word "Alaska" originated from the Aleutian language, which was spoken by the natives of the Aleutian Islands of Alaska. The Aleutian word is "aláxsxaq," which means "an object the sea is directed to" or "place the sea crashes against." In this instance, it refers to the Alaskan peninsula and mainland. The translation is sometimes considered to be "great land."

The Russians originally used the word "Alaska" only when they were referring to the peninsula. When the United States bought the territory from the Russians, they chose to adopt the name, too—but opted to use it to refer to the entire territory.

The Gold Rush Helped Increase the Population of Alaska

Did you know the "Alaskan Gold Rush" helped increase the region's population? Although the gold rush didn't last for a long time, it played a key role in the state's history.

The gold rush is actually formally known as the Klondike Gold Rush, though it's been nicknamed the Alaskan Gold Rush. This nickname isn't the best-suiting for the gold rush. While some gold was discovered in Alaska, most of the discoveries of gold were made in the Yukon and Canada. However, the best way to get to the Yukon was to travel through the Skagway in Alaska.

In Alaska itself, gold was first discovered in Juneau in 1880. In 1902, a second Alaskan gold rush began when gold was discovered in the Fairbanks region.

Over the course of 10 years, the Alaskan population greatly increased. In 1890, there was only a little more than 32,000 residents in the region. However, there were more than 63,000 people living in the area by 1900.

In 1916, the Alaska-Juneau gold mine was built. It was the largest gold mine in the entire world. Between the years of 1916 and 1944, the Alaska-Juneau gold mine produced more than $80 million worth of gold. The mine close in 1944 during World War II.

Alaska Has Had Two State Capitals — and Anchorage Wasn't One of Them

When the United States purchased Alaska from Russia, they kept the original capital that had been chosen by the Russians. The city was then called Novoarkhangelsk, or the New Archangel. When the United States acquired the region, they changed the name of Novoarkhangelsk to Sitka.

In 1906, the capital was moved to Juneau. Juneau was chosen because the Klondike Gold Rush had made the city an economic powerhouse.

People often question why Anchorage wasn't chosen as the capital. Anchorage, which is the northernmost city in the United States, has a population of about 300,000 people and is also home to over 41% of the state's population. When Juneau was chosen as the capital of Alaska, Anchorage wasn't founded yet. Anchorage wasn't formed until 1914 when it was selected as construction headquarters for the Alaska Railroad. Anchorage also didn't become a town of much importance until it became military headquarters, just prior to World War II.

Juneau was the capital when Alaska officially became a territory, and it remains the state's capital today!

Alaska Was Attacked After Pearl Harbor

You probably already know by now that the Japanese attacked Pearl Harbor. But did you know that Japan also attacked Alaska's Aleutian Islands?

Japan bombed Dutch Harbor in the Aleutian Islands in June of 1942, following the attack on Pearl Harbor. Forces also invaded the islands, Kiska and Attu, which they occupied for almost a year.

The United States Navy knew that the attack was an attempt at diverting their attention, so they didn't try very hard to defend the Aleutian Islands. As a result, more than 90 people were taken to Japan as prisoners of war.

In May of 1943, Americans fought back. They invaded the Japanese at Attu. American and Canadian forces planned an invasion on Kiska, but at that time, Japanese had already abandoned the area and withdrawn.

Today, there's an Aleutian World War II National Historic Area Visitors Center that tourists can visit if they want to learn more about the historical invasion. The center also helps visitors learn more about the Aleut natives in general.

How Alaska Got Its State Nickname

Have you ever wondered about Alaska's state nickname? Alaska is known as the "Last Frontier," but do you know why it came to be called this?

It's believed that the state of Alaska earned its nickname due to it consisting of a large amount of land that was never accurately mapped out or explored throughout the region. The harsh climate conditions in Alaska have made it difficult for the entire state to be explored thoroughly. Although there are cities and towns throughout the state, there are also a lot of remote and underdeveloped regions as well. To this day, the majority of Alaska's territory remains uncharted.

There's another theory as to why Alaska was nicknamed the Last Frontier. The state is said to be the "last frontier" for people who want to start a new life or business, thanks to the large amount of timber, minerals, and wildlife that can be hunted. The Alaska state government provides homesteading rights, mining claims, tax relief, and a number of other benefits to people who help bring industry to the state.

The Land of the Midnight Sun

While the Last Frontier is Alaska's official state nickname, it's also long been called the "Land of the Midnight Sun" as well. This unofficial state nickname has been given because the sun shines 24 hours a day during summer in Alaska and isn't seen for months at a time during the winter months. Even at midnight, the sun can still be seen during Alaskan summers.

The "longest night," or period of darkness, takes place

in Barrow, Alaska. This darkness lasts for 67 days. During the summer, the "longest day," or period of non-stop sunlight, lasts for a total of 82 days.

While Alaska is most well-known for its dark winters, don't let this fool you. Alaska actually sees more hours of sunlight between March 19th and September 23rd than any other state in the country! This makes it a great time for sightseeing, hiking, and golfing. In fact, golfing is often enjoyed until 10 p.m.

Thanks to the extra sunlight, Alaska is also known to produce larger than average vegetables. Many of the state's vegetables have set Guinness World Records. Some of the state's biggest vegetables on record include a 94-lb cabbage, 35-lb broccoli, and 31.25-lb cauliflower.

Another thing that's more common in Alaska due to the extra sunshine? Mosquitoes—*lots* of mosquitoes. Since the sun is shining 24 hours a day, it's said to cause the mosquitoes (and other bugs) to breed more than they normally would in a state where the sun goes down. If you're planning a trip to Alaska, you'll want to make sure you have plenty of bug spray on hand.

A Famous Hero Came Out of Alaska

One of the most famous American heroes in history came from Alaska. Do you know which one it is?

One hint: he's *not* human!

Balto is the famous Siberian Husky sled dog who led his team to deliver medicine to treat a diphtheria outbreak during a blizzard with temperatures as low as −23 °F in January of 1925. The medicine was transported by train from Anchorage to Nenana, Alaska. From there, Balto and his dog sled team carried the medicine to Nome, where the diphtheria outbreak was taking place.

Although Balto is widely regarded as the hero of the trip, there has been some controversy about who the true hero really is. Some consider another sled dog, named Togo, to be the real hero. Togo led his team through the first 200 miles of the trip, through strong winds and snow. The medicine was later passed to Norwegian Gunnar Kaasen, who drove Balto's team.

News of the miracle dog sled run made international headlines.

Today, you can see Togo's stuffed and preserved body at the Iditarod Trail Sled Dog Race Museum, which is located in Wasilla, Alaska. Balto's stuffed and preserved body is located at the Cleveland Museum of Natural History, however.

The 1995 animated film *Balto* is loosely based on Balto's real-life journey.

There's also a statue of Balto in Central Park in New York City that honors the legendary canine.

Historical Natural Disasters Have Taken Place in the State

When you think of natural disasters in the United States, Alaska might not be the first state that comes to mind. But did you know major natural disasters have taken place in Alaska? In fact, some of the most significant natural disasters in the world have occurred in the Last Frontier.

Earthquakes are fairly common in Alaska. Approximately 5,000 earthquakes take place in the state each year. This is more earthquakes on an annual basis than even California. The strongest earthquake to ever occur in North America took place in Alaska in March of 1964. The earthquake, which happened in Prince William Sound, had a magnitude of 9.2. Known as the 1964 Alaskan earthquake, it was the second most powerful earthquake to occur in the history of the entire world!

The earthquake, which lasted for 4.5 minutes, is believed to be responsible for about 139 deaths. Fifteen of these deaths occurred as a direct result of the earthquake itself, due to ground fissures and collapsed buildings throughout south-central Alaska, while the majority of the deaths were a result of the tsunamis caused by the earthquake. The tsunamis caused waves to other countries, including New Zealand, Japan, and Mexico! It's been estimated that

106 people died as a result of the tsunami in Alaska, with 13 deaths from the tsunami in California and 5 deaths from the tsunami in Oregon.

The earthquake caused $115 million (or an estimated $0.71 billion in 2016) worth of damage to the state. Since the earthquake occurred after 5 p.m. on Good Friday, it's believed that the damage could have been even worse than it was. Since it was the first natural disaster to ever really take place in the state, the Alaska state government wasn't prepared. The military in the state stepped in with disaster relief efforts.

The 1964 Alaskan earthquake isn't the only natural disaster that has ever taken place in the state. In June of 1912, the most powerful volcanic explosion to ever take place in the 20th century occurred when the Novarupta Volcano erupted. The Novarupta Volcano is located on the Alaskan peninsula in Katmai National Park.

An hour after the eruption took place, the blast was heard by residents of Juneau, Alaska, which is located more than 700 miles away from the volcano. The volcanic eruption sent tephra and gas into the atmosphere for 60 hours. Ash fell on the town during the hours following the eruption and fell for the next three days. The ash cloud rose 20 miles in elevation, before drifting to Kodiak, Alaska.

Once the eruption was over, the area was devastated by 30 cubic kilometers of ejecta. The amount of magma was over 30 times more than the 1980 Mount St. Helens eruption, as well as triple the amount of the 1991 Mount Pinatubo eruption, the second-largest volcanic explosion in the 20th century.

Despite how powerful the volcanic eruption was, it isn't believed to have caused any deaths.

Alaska is a Huge Oil Production State

When you think of petroleum-producing states in America, Texas is probably the first state that comes to mind. But did you know that Alaska is actually responsible for 25% of the oil that's produced in the United States?

The Alaska Pipeline at Prudhoe Bay produces an average of 10,000 barrels of oil a day. For comparison's sake, the average amount 48 of the other stations in the nation is only 11 barrels per day.

The Alaska Pipeline, which spans across 800 miles, has been a huge source of controversy. The pipeline was built in 1977 during an oil crisis. It's owned by a private company called the Alyeska Pipeline Company. In 1978, someone blew a tiny hole in the pipeline near Fairbanks, which caused 16,000 barrels to leak into the ocean. Then in 2001, a man named Daniel Lewis caused 6,000 barrels to leak out after he shot a hole in the pipeline, a crime which earned him 16 years in jail and a $17 million fine.

There was also the incident of the Exxon Valdez, which is otherwise known as the Oriental Nicety. It occurred in March of 1989 when an Exxon Valdez oil tanker was transporting crude oil from the Alaskan Pipeline. The tanker was running aground in Prince William Sound in route to Long Beach, California. Before it could get there, there was a huge oil spill. It's been estimated that 10.8 to 31.7 million gallons of oil were spilled in Alaska. It was the 54th largest oil spill in history.

Many have concerns over the toll the Alaska Pipeline has had on the environment, but despite its controversies, the Alaskan government relies solely on its royalties from oil production as the state doesn't collect individual income tax or sales tax. It is one of only five states that doesn't collect sales taxes and one of only seven states that doesn't collect individual income taxes. The state is also considered to be tax-friendly for businesses. Instead of taxes, Alaska's government is funded by its petroleum revenue and federal subsidies.

Alaska state residents get an "oil royalty check" each year, which gives them a percentage of their share of revenue accrued from the state's oil production. As of 2008, the check was a little over $2,000.

A Controversial Candidate for USA Vice President Came from Alaska

You probably know by now that Sarah Palin, who ran as vice president alongside former Republican presidential nominee, John McCain, is from Alaska. Palin has been the source of much controversy in United States politics. What you might not know is that Sarah Palin's Alaskan roots run deep.

While the former candidate was born in Idaho, her family moved to Alaska when she was just an infant. Palin attended Wasilla High School, where she played basketball. Today she's most well-known for her support of guns and the National Rifle Association, but Sarah Palin was also a beauty pageant queen at one time. In 1984, she was crowned Miss Wasilla and she was also a runner-up for Miss Alaska.

In 1996, Sarah Palin was elected as the Mayor of Wasilla. In 2006, she was elected as the 9th governor of Alaska. Not only was she the first female to ever become governor, but she was also the youngest! Palin resigned from her position as governor in 2009 in order to run alongside John McCain.

Many have blamed Sarah Palin as the reason why McCain's presidential run was unsuccessful. While she was popular among some conservatives, many Americans did not agree with some of Palin's extreme views. Comedian Tina Fey also did a portrayal of Sarah Palin on *Saturday Night Live*, which is believed to have further hurt McCain and Palin's bid for office.

Alaska is the Largest State in the Entire Country

You've probably heard that Alaska is a big state, but do you know just *how* big it is? The only way to truly appreciate the state's size is to see it for yourself, but let's talk numbers.

Alaska encompasses 375 million miles or 591,000 square acres of land, making it the largest U.S. state. Alaska is 1/5 the size of the entire United States. It's also larger than the size of Texas, the second largest state in the country. In fact, if you include Alaska's territorial waters, the state is larger than the three largest states in the country: Texas, California, and Montana—*combined*. The state could fit a total of 19 U.S. states inside its borders, while the state of Rhode Island could fit into Alaska more than 400 times!

Spanning across 3,108 square miles, Juneau is also (unsurprisingly) the largest state capital in the United States. Juneau is larger than the states of Delaware and Rhode Island separately, and *almost* as large as the two states combined.

Fun Bonus Fact: Juneau was named after gold prospector Joe Juneau. Prior to that, the city had been called Rockwell and Harrisburg (after Richard Harris, another gold prospector who had close ties to Joe Juneau). And even before that, the Tlingit tribe had called the city Dzántik'i Héeni, which means "river where the flounders gather."

Alaska Doesn't Have a Lot of Connected Roads (Or Many Roads at All, For That Matter)

Did you know that Alaska doesn't have a lot of connected roads in comparison to the rest of the United States?

Of course, this makes sense. If Alaska had a widely connect road system, then most of the state would have been better explored by now and it wouldn't still be known as the Last Frontier. What you might not realize, however, is just how much the state lacks a complete road system or how remote most of the state is.

The Alaska state road system only covers a small portion of the state. In fact, most of the state doesn't have roads *at all*. There are roads which link the Alaska Highway, which leads into Canada. There are also roads in Southeast Alaska, near Anchorage and Fairbanks, which is where the majority of the state's population resides.

There isn't a road system that connects Western or most of Northern Alaska to the rest of the state, meaning the communities in this region are extremely remote and desolate.

Nome, Alaska is the largest settlement in the United States, but there are no roads to get there. There has been talk for literally decades about building a road to Nome, but it has yet to be seen. There are also no roads to Barrow, Alaska, which is the northernmost city in the United States and a popular tourist attraction.

What might surprise you most is that even Juneau, Alaska can't be accessed by road. It's the only capital city in the country that can't be accessed by car. The only way to get to the state's capital is by plane or ferry. This has even led many to question if the capital should be moved, but it hasn't happened yet.

This all begs the question: why are there no roads in most of Alaska?

Most of the answer comes down to the state's climate. Most of Alaska is permafrost, which makes roadbuilding complicated, to say the least. In the summer, the frozen soil expands, which would cause pavement to develop cracks. Permafrost remains solid throughout winter, but it ends up turning into muddy swamps during the summer months. These are less than ideal conditions for road construction.

It has been said that water is the best highway to Alaska since most travel is done by water. In the winter, frozen rivers—especially the Yukon River—

are one of the best ways to travel. People have taken dog sleds on them, walked them by foot (sometimes causing them to die), and rode their bicycles on them. Air travel is also common among both tourists and residents. In fact, there are known to be more private plane owners in Alaska than any other state in the country! It makes sense why.

Hopefully, a larger road system will be built in the state in the future, but right now it seems like nothing more than a pipe dream.

You Can Pan for Gold When You Visit Alaska

The Klondike Gold Rush might be over, but that doesn't mean you can't still go gold mining today. In fact, it's It's been estimated that only 1% of Alaska's gold has yet to be discovered, meaning there is a lot of gold still left to be found! The question is: will *you* find it? There are a number of places in the Last Frontier where you can try your hand at searching for gold.

A popular place for tourists to go gold panning is Nome Creek in White Mountains National Recreation Area. The region has a strong history of gold mining. You can check out the Maze, which was formed by the gold-mining dredge. Today, tourists can go panning for gold in the recreational area.

Some other places where you might find gold in

Alaska include Caribou Creek Recreational Mining Area or Petersville Recreational Mining Area.

At the Chicken Gold Camp & Outpost, you can learn a whole lot more about the gold mining experience. Located in Chicken, Alaska, Chicken Gold Camp & Outpost is located on the site of a former gold camp from the 1930s. It's also home to a Pedro Dredge, which is a bucket line gold dredge that's been named a National Historic Site. You'll get to experience an actual working gold mine, tour the mining museum, mine or pan for gold, and so much more!

It's important to keep in mind that most of these areas only allow you to go recreational gold mining. The most you might be able to take home with you are some gold nuggets. These areas don't allow you to stake mining claims, which is to prevent any conflict between mining claim owners and the general public.

RANDOM FACTS

1. There's a popular myth that men in Alaska outnumber women by 10 to 1. While this isn't true, your chances of finding a man in Alaska are still pretty good if you're a woman. Alaska is the state with the highest male to female ratio. It's been estimated that approximately 52% of the state's population is male and that there are about 107 men for every 100 women in the Last Frontier.

2. Alaska has the lowest population density of any state in the USA, as well as one of the lowest population densities in all of America. The population density is approximately 1.26 people per square mile. It has been estimated that if Manhattan had the same population density as Alaska, there would only be 27 people living in the city, instead of its 1.6 million. Alaska also has the third lowest overall population out of any state in the U.S.

3. Tex Rickard was a gambler who became famous in the saloons of Circle City, Alaska back in the 1890s. Rickard was drawn to the area by the Klondike Gold Rush where he found gold. He sold his gold for $60,000 and opened a saloon,

hotel, and gambling hall in Yukon, Canada. He ended up gambling everything away, including his share of the Northern. He went on to promote boxing matches, which led him to have a lifelong friendship with Wyatt Earp, who was a boxing fan and officiant. The two even stayed in touch until Rickard became ill before his death. Earp died the same month. Rickard later built Madison Square Garden in New York City. He was also the founder of the NHL's the New York Rangers.

4. While the famous saying "I can see Russia from my house," which Tina Fey made while impersonating Sarah Palin on *Saturday Night Live*, isn't true, Alaska really isn't all that far away from Russia. The state is located less than 50 miles away from the country. One point of Alaska—Little Diomede Island—is located just 2.4 miles away from Russia's Big Diomede Island.

5. A thirteen-year-old boy named Benny Benson designed the Alaska state flag. Back in 1927, students in the then-territory were asked to submit their ideas for Alaska's flag. Benson's design of the Big Dipper and North Star was the idea that was chosen.

6. Like other U.S. states, Alaska is home to a number of strange laws—several of which are moose-themed. It's illegal to give a moose beer, view a moose from a plane, and, most strangely,

push a moose from a plane. It's also illegal to whisper in someone's ear while they are moose hunting. If you're thinking about waking up a sleeping bear to photograph it, you should know that's also against the law. In Juneau, if you have a pet flamingo, you can't take it to a barber shop. In Anchorage, you can't tie your pet dog to the roof of your car or live in a trailer while it's being hauled across the city.

7. When you hit an animal on the Alaska State Highway, don't think about taking your roadkill home. When bear, moose, reindeer, and caribou are killed by cars in Alaska, the road kill is considered the property of the state. What does the state do with it, you wonder? Reported road kill is butchered by volunteers and later distributed as food to charity organizations throughout the state. Hundreds of animals are donated to charities each year, which helps low-income families survive Alaska's harsh winters.

8. The Alaskan Claims Settlement Act, or ANCSA, is the largest compensation to ever be awarded to any United States natives in history. Established in 1971, the act provided a billion dollars and 40 million acres of land to American citizens with at least 25% Inuit, Aleut, or Athabascan blood.

9. The first civil rights legislation act in the United States was passed in Alaska in 1945. Alaska's

Nondiscrimination Act of 1945 came into existence just weeks before New York's non-discrimination act. The act was created to protect natives from being banned from public locations and excluded from trade and employment opportunities.

10. Wyatt Earp may be famous for his roots in the western United States, but did you know that he also spent some time in Alaska, too? In fact, back in 1867, Wyatt Earp even served as the sheriff of Wrangell, Alaska for 10 days. Earp came into this position when he and his wife were passing through the town on their way to the Klondike.

11. Alaska is home to the largest combination rail and highway tunnel in all of North America. The Anton Anderson Memorial Tunnel is also the second longest highway tunnel in North America. The single-lane tunnel runs beneath Maynard Mountain.

12. The Alaskan Independence Party is a group of Alaskan citizens who believe the state should separate from the United States. They feel the citizens weren't given a fair chance to vote or choose statehood, commonwealth status, or succession from the rest of the United State. As of 2009, the Alaskan Independence Party had more than 13,000 registered members and was the third largest party in the state.

13. While Hawaii might be the first state that comes to mind when it comes to expensive goods, things cost a lot in Alaska as well. This is due to the harsh climate conditions, remote locations, and lack of a transportation infrastructure. People who live in rural areas are most affected by these prices. Foods staples, such as bread and milk, are often double the cost of what they are in other states. Alaska's gas prices are also generally 20 to 30 cents more on average than in other states. The only state with higher gas prices than Alaska is Hawaii. Since basic goods cost so much more in Alaska, most federal government employees earn 25% more than they do in other states to make up the difference.

14. A tragic fact about Alaska is that the state's known as the rape capital of the United States. Sadly, the state's rape rate is more than double the national average. Child sexual assaults are also six times higher than the national average. The majority of these crimes occur in rural areas, which don't have a lot of law enforcement. It's believed that the numbers may actually be even worse than they appear since it's thought that many of the crimes are kept secrets within the community that don't ever get reported.

15. The entire town of Whittier, Alaska lives in one building. Begich Towers, or BTI, was originally

designed to be a military base during the Cold War. However, the plans fell through when it was determined that it was too remotely located. Today, its apartments are home to Whittier's 200 residents. A school, a grocery store, a post office, a video store, a church, a healthcare center, and city offices can also be found within BTI. The benefit of this arrangement is that the town's residents don't have to battle the cold temperatures to get to school, work or the grocery store during winter.

16. Airport Pizza just may have the most innovative pizza delivery service in the country. The restaurant delivers pizza by plane throughout the state of Alaska. Located in Nome, Alaska, deliveries have been made as far as 200 miles away! The best part about it all is that the restaurant doesn't charge people hundreds of dollars for these deliveries. A pizza only costs $30, regardless of delivery location.

17. People who are looking to find work in Alaska might want to consider the seafood and fishing industry, which is the largest private employment industry in the state. In fact, the majority of the United State's salmon, herring, halibut, and crab comes from the state. Approximately 95% of the U.S.'s supply of salmon comes from the state. It's worth noting, however, that Alaska's commercial

fishing industry is considered the most dangerous job industry in not only the United States but the entire world. This is due to the harsh weather and water conditions. Rogue waves, icy ship decks, and extremely cold waters make fishing in the region more dangerous than it is throughout the rest of the world. As of 2007, there were 128 fatalities for every 100,000 fishermen in Alaska, which is 26 times higher than the United States average, according to the National Institute for Occupational Safety and Health. Additionally, one out of three of all work-related fatalities in the state is caused by commercial fishing.

18. A cat was once mayor of Talkeetna, Alaska. The cat, who was named Stubbs, served as mayor from July of 1997 until he died in July of 2017. Stubbs the cat was considered one of the town's biggest tourist attractions, with approximately 30 to 40 tourists stopping in to meet him every day as they were traveling to other nearby towns. Talkeetna doesn't actually have a mayor or an election, so Stubbs' position as mayor was only honorary. His "mayoral office" was at Nagley's General Store, where his owner, Lauri Stec, was a manager.

19. Alaska is home to a number of nature's wonders. Seventeen of the 20 highest peaks in the United States can be found in Alaska. The state is home

to more than 100 volcanoes and volcanic fields, all of which have been active within the past 2 million years. Over 3,000 rivers and 3 million lakes can be found in Alaska—including the largest, Lake Iliamna, which is said to be approximately the same size as the entire state of Connecticut. More than 50% of the glaciers in the entire world can be found in the state. In fact, the state is home to more than 1,000 glaciers.

20. Alaska has 34,000 miles of coastline, which is more than the rest of the U.S. states' coastlines *combined*. It's also the only state that has coastlines which are located on three different seas: the Bering Sea, the Pacific Ocean, and the Arctic Ocean.

Test Yourself – Questions and Answers

1. Which language did the name "Alaska" originate from?

    a. Russian
    b. Norwegian
    c. Aleutian

2. Which heroic animal came from Alaska?

    a. Sergeant Stubby
    b. Balto
    c. Moko the dolphin

3. The Alaskan earthquake, which was the strongest to ever occur in North America, happened in which year?

    a. 1964
    b. 1962
    c. 1954

4. The point in Alaska which is located closest to Russia is how many miles away?

    a. 10 miles away
    b. 2.4 miles away
    c. 3 miles away

5. The 13-year-old boy who designed the Alaska state flag was named:

    a. Benny Benson
    b. Benson Ben
    c. Benny Harding

Answers

1. c.
2. b.
3. a.
4. b.
5. a.

CHAPTER TWO

ALASKA'S "ESKIMOS": THE NATIVES AND THEIR CULTURE

Alaska's natives play a key role in the state's culture. Today, there are about 200 native villages in all of Alaska. But what do you really know about Alaskan native culture? Do you know what an "Eskimo kiss" is or what it really signifies? One hint: it actually has nothing to do with kissing. Do you know where the term "Eskimo" originated from or what it means today? Do you know what surprising bear Alaska's natives historically hunted and still continue to hunt to this day? To find out these and other facts about Alaska's natives, read on!

Alaska's Native Groups

When you hear the word "Eskimo," you might think it only applies to one group of people. However, this couldn't be further from the truth. Eskimos are made up of a number of different cultural groups. These include the following:

- **The Inuit** – This group of people originally lived in western Alaska, relying almost solely on sea animals for food, oil, clothing, and more. Their diets included very few plants. As they moved eastwards, they began to hunt land animals and began to make tools and weapons out of antlers, bones, and other animal by-products. The Inuit have been widely regarded as expert hunters. The word "Inuit" means "the people" or "real people" in Inuktitut, the language that was spoken by the Inuit.

- **The Aleut** – This native group occupied what is now known as the Aleutian Islands, which is located about 1,000 miles west of the Alaskan mainland. The name "Aleut" originated from the Russians. While they are known as the Aleut today, the tribe actually refers to themselves as the "Unangas" and the "Sugpiaq." The name the "Aleutian Islands" means "the land of the Aleut" and was also derived from the Russians. The Aleut spent most of their time hunting at the sea, but they also did some hunting and gathering on land as well. Famous for their basketry, they were talented fishers and hunters. It's believed that the Aleut's ancestors migrated to the area about 7,000 years ago.

- **The Athabascan (or Athapascan)** – Traditionally found in the northern boreal forest, this Alaskan native group lived primarily off natural resources. Due to harsher living conditions, the Athabascan experienced more famine than other Alaskan native groups, who were able to live off sea animals. The Athabascan is said to have a deep respect for Alaska's land and its animals. This group has been around for thousands of years.
- **The Yupik (or Yu'pik)** – This group was most often found in western and southwestern Alaska, but they were also found throughout southcentral Alaska as well. The word "Yu'pik" originates from the Yu'pik words, "yuk," which means "person," and "pik," which means "real" or "genuine." Thus, the meaning of the word "Yu'pik" is "real person." During the winter, Yupik families traditionally lived in the villages. In spring, they tended to go off in their separate ways to camps they made for fishing.
- **The Inupiat** – This indigenous group has called Alaska home for more than 10,000 years, which is when their Siberian ancestors first crossed the Bering Land Bridge. They lived in camps, villages, and trading groups. They gathered berries, fished, and hunted whales, caribou, and moose.
- **The Tlingit** – Found primarily in Southeast

Alaska, this group of people is believed to have originated from Asia and Japan. This theory is based on the similarities between their artwork. Unlike the other native groups, the Tlingit focused more on trading and crafting than they did on survival techniques.

These groups only account for six of the eleven Alaskan native groups. That being said, these groups are the most well-known.

Where the Term "Eskimo" Came From

The Alaskan Inuit, Aleut, Yupik, and the other Alaskan natives mentioned above are often referred to as "Eskimos". Have you ever wondered where the term "Eskimo" originated from?

The word "Eskimo" comes from the French word Esquimau, which originated from the Algonquin word "askimowew." Askimowew has long been said to translate to "eater of raw meat." Some linguistics, however, believe that the term actually originated from an Ojibwa word meaning "to net snowshoes."

Wherever the word "Eskimo" came from, Alaskan natives don't like that they've been defined by outsiders. For that reason, "Eskimo" is now considered a derogatory and culturally insensitive term. It's often compared to using "Indians" when referring to America's Native Americans. Although most Americans don't realize "Eskimo" is considered derogatory, the native people may become offended by it.

So, what do you use in place of "Eskimo"? Inuit (for multiple people) and Inuk (for one person) are also considered acceptable terms for this population of people, even though not all natives are Inuit. It's also acceptable to use the term "Alaskan native," since it can be used to describe natives who aren't Inuit. This is the best option to use if you don't know the actual tribe of the native you're speaking to or about.

Alaskan Natives Don't Really Have Hundreds of Words for "Snow"

A common misconception that's been widely accepted by Americans is that the Alaskan natives have hundreds of words for snow. In fact, some say there are up to 500 different words to describe snow. This actually couldn't be further from the truth.

While there are a lot of Inuit phrases that can be used to describe weather conditions, there are actually only three words that mean snow. The word "aqilokoq" translates to "softly falling snow." This is the most commonly used Inuit term for snow.

So, where did this myth about the Inuit come from? During the 19th century, an anthropologist by the name of Franz Boas lived with the Inuit to learn more about their culture. He noted that the Inuit frequently referred to the snow, but it was a misunderstanding of their sentence structure that caused this confusion for him.

The Truth About Natives Living in Igloos

When you think of where "Eskimos" live, igloos are probably the first thing that comes to mind. Well, this is true… but *only* because "igloo" means "house" in the Inuit language. It's only outside of the Inuit culture that "igloo" is used to describe huts that are made from snow blocks.

The truth is that Alaska's natives don't live in snow huts today. In fact, most of them live in traditional houses. Some native Alaskans also have a different version of the igloo that they call home, which they construct from wood and whale bone. They use seal skin for the roof and insulation. Although these "igloos" were more common in the past, some natives still live in them today.

Igloos were invented to provide people with warmth during their hunting trips. During the harsh winters, the natives would travel to areas near the sea, where they would go to hunt seals. The igloos they stayed in during those times only provided temporary shelter, since the snow melts when summer comes. Some Alaskan native hunters only lived in their igloos for a few days, while others stayed in them throughout the entire winter. Some of Alaska's natives continue to use igloos for hunting trips today.

The size of igloos varied. Some igloos were designed for just one person who was hunting, while others were designed for one or more families.

You might be wondering how the snow and ice used to build an igloo is enough to keep someone warm, but experts say a good igloo can increase temperatures 40 degrees Fahrenheit from whatever the outdoor temperature is. There are several reasons. The walls help to block the wind, which is one of the coldest parts about Alaskan winters. The snow and ice of the igloo become insulators, trapping body heat inside the igloo. An oil lamp or a fire is also typically used within the igloo to heat things up.

In the summer, Alaska natives lived in tents or houses they made from a combination of animal skin, wood, and/or bones. The type of skin they would use depended on where they lived in the summer. Caribou and bear skin was used for natives who lived inland, while seal skin was typically used for those who lived near the ocean.

An "Eskimo Kiss" Probably Isn't What You Think It Is

You've probably heard of an "Eskimo kiss," which happens when two people rub their noses together as a gesture of affection. But do you know what it is?

Most people think this is an Inuit's way of kissing, but you couldn't be more wrong.

The "Eskimo kiss" is actually called the "kunik." It might surprise you to learn that while this is an intimate gesture that does take place between couples, it actually has *nothing* to do with kissing. It's typically done in private, but it's also a gesture that's common among family members as well.

Although it may look like they are just rubbing their noses together, they're actually sniffing each other's hair and cheeks (where there are sweat glands, which give off a scent). The purpose is so that two people who haven't seen each other in a while can be reminded of each other's scent.

Alaskan Natives Hunt This Type of Bear

Have you ever wondered what Inuit and other Alaskan natives eat? One of the types of meat they ate just might surprise you.

Alaska's indigenous took part in what is now known as a practice called "subsistence." The practice of finding subsistence foods, which allowed the Alaskan natives to live off the land and survive harsh winters, is a practice that many natives still take part in today. What does this mean, exactly?

Throughout history, the Alaskan natives primarily hunted and fished for their food. In fact, they're known to be great hunters who can capture just about any animal. While some native groups did gather plants, these weren't always easy for some groups to find based on their location. They also needed to preserve their plants through the harsh Alaskan winters, which meant that most groups still primarily focused on hunting to sustain their diets.

Although modernization has led to a shift towards a westernized diet, many still continue to live off the meat they hunt. Some still participate in it for cultural reasons, while others hunt because this is the way of life they choose.

Some of the most common animals that Alaska's indigenous groups have hunted throughout history and continue to hunt today include caribou (reindeer), moose, mountain sheep, walruses, and seals. They use seal oil for preparing their food. But one of the most historically prized hunts among Inuit and other natives may surprise you: polar bears!

Polar bears, which are called "Nanuq" in the Inuit language, were historically believed to be the most mighty and powerful bears. They were even considered "almost human."

According to Polar Bears International:

"Legend held that if a dead polar bear was treated properly by the hunter, it would share the good news with other bears so they would be eager to be killed by him. Bears would stay away from hunters who failed to pay respect."

To pay their respect to the bear, the hunter would hang the bear's hide in their igloo for a few days. They would also offer tools to the bear's spirit as a gift. The Alaskan natives would then use all of the bear's meat (aside from the liver, which is toxic to humans and even sled dogs) and use the animal's fur to make trousers and soft boots.

Today, Alaskan natives continue to hunt polar bears. Since the polar bear population has been decreasing in recent times, however, these hunts are carefully regulated. The U.S. Fish & Wildlife Service grants polar bear hunting rights to people of Alaskan native heritage, due to the cultural significance of the practice. It's illegal for anyone else in the state besides native to hunt polar bears. Although there is no limit on the number of polar bears an Alaskan may hunt throughout the year, all hunts must be reported. All meat must be used and can be sold to another native or native village. The polar bear's fur can also be used in Alaskan Native handcrafts to sell.

The Natives Made Armor for Hunting

When you think of hunting, you might not typically think of armor, but the Inupiat used armor when they went hunting. This is because many of the animals they hunted—including polar bears—are very dangerous creatures. The armor helped keep them protected from their prey.

The Alaskan natives were also very skilled at making armor. They constructed it out of bone, usually from walrus ivory. They would strap the armor together with leather. The Alaskan native version of armor is very similar to the armor that was made by ancient Japanese time.

The Alaskan natives also handcrafted their own hunting weapons and tools from whale bone, antlers, and more. We'll talk more about some of their most well-known inventions a later chapter.

European Settlement Caused Devastation Among Alaska's Natives

A little-known fact about Alaska's culture is that the natives experienced a lot of devastation thanks to European settlers. Just like with the Native Americans throughout the rest of the United States, European settlement wasn't without problems for Alaska's indigenous populations.

When the Europeans arrived in Alaska during the 1800s, they brought many diseases with them. There was an epidemic of tuberculosis, as well as influenza, the measles, and smallpox. The Alaskan natives' immune systems weren't used to these diseases, which led to many deaths. In some cases, entire villages died off. Others were greatly affected, despite some surviving members. It's been estimated that almost 90% of the Inuit population died as a result of European illnesses.

In addition, the European settlers killed many of the Alaskan natives. They also indirectly led to their deaths. The Europeans began to hunt whales and other animals the natives lived on, making it harder for them to hunt and leading them to starve to death.

The Europeans are also often blamed for the destruction of Alaska native traditions. While some traditions have managed to survive the test of time, many died with the arrival of settlers.

The Europeans aren't the only ones who caused harm to the Inuit and other natives. The Vikings also killed the natives they encountered for no reason.

The Alaskan Natives Were the First to Use Dog Sleds

Have you ever wondered who the first to use dog sleds were? If you guessed Alaska's natives, then you're spot on! The Inuit and other natives are credited with inventing the first dog sleds. However, these sleds aren't necessarily what you would picture today.

The exact design of dog sleds tended to vary widely between the actual tribe and the region they lived in. That being said, there were some common factors between designs.

Known as a "qamutiik," the first dog sleds weren't

built with nails or pins. Each piece was drilled and lashed to the next to make it more flexible so that it could move across heavy ice and snow more easily.

While some of the first sleds were made from wood, it wasn't always readily available, depending on where the natives lived. When wood wasn't an option, the natives would use frozen fish that they wrapped in animal skins instead. The sleds were also made from whale bones.

The first dog sleds were designed for hunting purposes. Many of the natives would travel long distances for their hunts. The sleds not only helped get them there, but it also helped them bring heavy loads of the animals they killed back home.

While the design of the sled itself played a key role in this form was very important, there was something that was even more significant: the sled dogs themselves.

A lot of strategic planning went into choosing the most effective dog team. Most believed that males made for the best pack leader, but some felt that females were a good choice—especially if a female dog was leading her own pups. It was generally accepted that dogs who were siblings tended to make a better team. Different tribes and different individuals held beliefs of their own on whether aggressive or calm dogs made the best leaders.

There were also certain breeds that were commonly chosen by Alaskan natives for sled dogs.

These Dog Breeds Were Commonly Used as Sled Dogs in Alaska

There are a few dog breeds that the Inuit and other native tribes used to pull their dog sleds. These include the Alaskan Malamute, the Siberian Husky, and the Alaskan Husky. All three of these dogs descended from Siberia's Chukotka sled dogs.

The Siberian Husky is said to be the result of Alaska's natives breeding dogs—likely Chukotka sled dogs—with wolves. The natives allegedly did this to produce stronger sled dogs.

You might think the word "Husky" originated from the Alaskan natives, but you'd be wrong. Surprisingly, it came from the English. The word "Husky" is short for "huskimos," which was a way the English sailors pronounced the word "Eskimos." The first use of the word was recorded back in 1852. At that time, the "Husky" was known as a "dog kept by the Inuit people."

The Alaskan Malamute is said to be the largest and oldest of all the sled dogs. It might not surprise you to learn that Alaska's official state dog is the Alaskan Malamute, a decision that was made due to the breed's role in the state's history. Not only is it a popular breed for dog sled racing, but it's also one of the breeds used most frequently in history to transport goods, by both the natives and other Alaskans.

Although these dog breeds can be found throughout the rest of the country today, they still remain commonplace in Alaska.

When visiting Alaskan villages today, some tourists might have the urge to try to pet the sled dogs. However, it's important to keep in mind that many of these dogs aren't trained to be petted or confronted by visitors. Although the dogs that roam the villages might look cute, many of them aren't tame. In some villages, sled dogs aren't treated as pets but as a means of transportation. Before petting a sled dog, it's best to ask the natives if it's safe to do so beforehand.

The Alaskan Natives Celebrated Holidays

You might not think that Alaska's natives celebrated holidays, but they did. There were several holiday festivals that the Inupiat held throughout the year.

During the spring season, there was "nalukataq," or the spring whaling festival. It took place after the whale hunt and was celebrated as a thanksgiving of sorts. The natives would ask for good luck with the following year's whaling hunt.

The nalukataq festival was also held in honor of the spirits of the whales and other sea animals they had hunted. The idea was to set free all of the spirits they had killed that hunting season. There was also a blanket toss that took place during the nalukataq festival. A walrus-skin trampoline was constructed and members of the tribe were bounced on it.

There was another spring festival that was held in honor of the coming of the sun. The natives would dress in costumes and dance to welcome the sun returning.

The Messenger Feast, which was known as "Kivgiq," was held in December. It may surprise you to learn that this feast involved social status and wealth. A messenger would travel to the neighboring community and invite it to attend the feast. The goal was usually to maintain or better a trading relationship with the other community. Gifts would be exchanged at the feast.

There were also trading fairs that the natives held throughout the years. The largest was the Kotzebue Fair, which took place in the summer.

Many of the Inupiat festivals were discouraged and died out due to Presbyterian missionaries who tried to eliminate native culture and ceremonies. There are still some that are celebrated today, however.

The Messenger Feast was re-established in 1988. It's

held in Barrow, Alaska in late January or February of most years. The purpose of the feast is to help inspire Alaskan natives with a stronger ethnic identity and a sense of native pride.

The Kotzebue Fair, which was brought back in 1991, is still celebrated today at Kobuk Valley National Park today. There are potlucks, performances, food, fashion, fur, and more at the parade, which takes place in early July of each year.

A Husband Had to Win His Wife's Family's Approval Before Marriage

Traditionally, a young Inupiat man had to woo a young woman's family before he could marry her. In most tribes, this meant the man would join the woman's father for hunting activities for a year or so prior to the marriage. Sometimes, the man would live with the woman's family until he had gained her family's acceptance.

Once he had the approval of the family—and especially the father—the young man would then be given permission to marry the young woman.

There were no formal marriage ceremonies. Instead, the bride and groom's "marriage" began when they started a sex life with one another.

In some cases, marriages were arranged by families when their children were just infants. At times, the community even forced it on the infants' parents.

The Inuit Had Many Legends

There are a number of myths and legends that the Inuit believed in. Some of the most popular Inuit myths include:

- **The legend of the Sea Goddess** – Known as the myth of Sedna or Taleelayuk (or Taluliyuk), this legend says that a young girl was cast into the ocean. She became the Sea Goddess or the keeper of all the sea mammals.
- **The legend of Lumiuk** – This legend involves a young abused blind boy. The boy ends up finding a safe haven in the sea, which helps him recover his vision and put an end to his abuse.
- **The legend of Tikta'liktak** – This myth tells the tale of a young hunter who gets lost on an isolated ice island. It involves his story of coming home.
- **The legend of Mahaha** – The Inuit believed in Mahaha, a demon that terrorized people living in the Arctic and who would kill anyone who crossed his path. His preferred method of killing? Tickling his victims to death.
- **The legend of the Tuniit** – The legend of these spirits says that they were the Inuit's ancestors. They possessed warrior-like strength, but they were also very simpleminded.

- **The legend of the Raven** – In one traditional tale told by the Inuit, the raven used to be white. It made a deal with the loon. The two birds are said to have tattooed one another, which led them to fling soot at each other. The story says this is what caused the raven's feathers to turn black and the loon's feathers to turn gray.

These are just some of the most popular legends of the Inuit. We'll touch on more Inuit and Alaskan native myths and legends in Chapter Six.

Alaskan Native Artwork

Alaskan tourists are drawn to the artwork produced by its natives—and for good reason. A lot of talent and craftsmanship goes into producing Native artwork. Here are some of the types of artwork that you can expect to find for sale when you visit Alaska:

- Carvings and masks that depict people and animals. These carvings may be made from ivory, soapstone, marine animal bone, and alabaster.
- Handwoven baskets, which may be made from baleen derived from the jaws of baleen whales and ivory.
- Dolls. Eskimo dolls, in particular, are popular. Dolls often depict styles and traditions of the artist's tribe. Dolls and their clothing may be made of caribou hide, mink, badger, sea otter,

seals, beavers, and other animals. Fur from wolves, musk ox, and other animals may also be used. Ivory may be used for the doll's eyes.

- Prints. A number of screen-printing techniques are used to create prints, which often depict designs, animals, and other things found in nature.

If you're ever in Alaska and considering buying Alaskan native artwork, it's suggested that you ask for proof of authentication. It's also important to remember that the price of artwork is often reflective of the amount of time that was put into handcrafting the item.

Modern Day Alaskan Natives

To this day, there are still many Alaskan natives living in Alaska. According to a U.S. Census in 2010, Alaskan natives accounted for about 15% of the overall Alaskan population.

However, modernization has changed the way of life for many of the natives. Today, there are permanent villages that some Alaskan natives continue to reside in. Others have chosen to leave the remote villages and traditional nomadic way of life, however. They've instead opted to live in towns and cities where they most often work in oil fields and mines. Some hold government jobs. Others work in arts and crafts.

Many of their modern weapons, such as harpoons and bows and arrows, have been replaced with rifles. While this makes hunting easier, it also has affected the Alaskan native culture.

Technology has also changed the way of life for many natives. Even in the most remote Alaskan native villages, there is generally television, phones, and nearby Internet access. Sled dogs have been replaced by snowmobiles, for the most part.

The Alaska Native Claims Settlement Act of 1971 provided $1 billion and gave the natives rights to approximately 10% of the state's land. This has also helped make the natives not need an entirely nomadic lifestyle in order for survival, though many choose to participate in nomadic practices for cultural reasons.

RANDOM FACTS

1. Alaska's natives have traditionally had an egalitarian society. Men were the hunters and fishers, while women completed domestic tasks, such as taking care of the children, cooking, and tanning hides. Other female tasks included gathering firewood, building igloos in winter, pitching tents in summer, and tanning animal hides. All people were believed to be important contributing members of the society, and all were viewed as essential for their survival. Women traditionally ate after men and guests, but one saying that illustrates the importance of women in Alaskan native society goes like this: "A hunter is what his wife makes him."

2. A lot of intermarriages took place between the Aleut and the Russian and European settlers. This is considered to be the reason why there aren't very many full-blooded Aleut in Alaska today.

3. Inuit are typically yellow-skinned people with black, coarse hair. On average, most of them tend to be about 5'4" in height. However, an Inuit group that was made up of tall, blonde people who appeared to be Scandinavian was

discovered in 1912. Although scientists initially thought the group was descendants of Vikings who had settled in the area, a DNA test that was performed in 2003 proven this theory to be wrong.

4. Aside from English, there are 20 native languages spoken in the state of Alaska. Some of these languages are only spoken by a few elders. In 2014, Alaska was the second state in the entire country to recognize indigenous languages as official languages. More than 5% of Alaska's residents speak at least one of its native languages. However, it has been estimated that Alaskan native languages may be extinct by 2100.

5. Any time the Inuit hunted an animal, they would sing songs, dance, and perform other traditional rituals to honor the spirit of the animal.

6. Traditional Alaskan native marriages were often not monogamous. It was extremely common for polygamy to exist within tribes, with one man taking more than one wife. This was a symbol of wealth or being a good provider. It was also common for men and women to swap partners, sometimes for enjoyment and other times due to one partner being infertile.

7. Traditionally, the Aleut tribe got tattoos and piercings. They believed these displays of body art would be pleasing to animal spirits and ward off any evil.

8. Today, the Inuit and other Alaskan native groups tend to experience some of the worst poverty levels in the United States. Alaskan natives earn only *half* of what Alaskan workers earn on average. In 2004, the U.S. Census Bureau found that the Alaskan native poverty rate was 16.1%, which is 3% higher than the national poverty rate.

9. When the Inuit went hunting for whales, they would generally go in a large group, usually consisting of at least 20 men. They would travel on a large boat called an Umiak. After they harpooned and killed the whale, they would tie it to the boat and drag it back to shore. Although it usually took a long time to kill a whale, it turned out to be worth it. A large whale provided enough meat to feed a small Inuit community for an entire year. The Inuit also used the whale's skin, oil, blubber, and bones.

10. Even though their diets are primarily meat and fat-based, consisted of very few plants, and lacked both dairy and grains or carbohydrates, the traditional Inuit diet is said to be one of the healthiest diets in the world. The high-protein,

high-fat diet the Inuit and other natives ate has been referred to as "the original Atkins Diet." However, the diets are different, with 50% of the Inuit diet coming from fats from wild game animals. It's believed that these fats, and particularly the Omega-3s they contain, are beneficial to the heart and vascular system.

11. The majority of the Alaskan natives who live in the state today speak English in addition to their own native languages. They are also generally given both a traditional Alaskan native name, as well as an English name, at birth.

12. When Russia sold the state in the Alaska Purchase, they didn't ask the natives first. At the time, there were less than 800 natives living in Alaska. Meanwhile, there were more than 3,000 Alaskan natives in the state.

13. An often talked about fact about Alaskan native society is that they would "kill off" elder members of the society, who were deemed "worthless." It's important to keep in mind that this isn't *entirely* true or as prevalent as many believe it to be. The tribe's elders were viewed as some of the most valuable members since they were wise and full of important knowledge. However, the Alaskan natives have been known to strangle, suffocate, or leave an

elder on a path when they became too difficult to care for. Sometimes, the elder asked to die but this wasn't always the case.

14. Although Christian missionaries converted many of Alaska's natives to their religion, the traditional religious beliefs were and still are practiced by many natives today. The religious beliefs of the Alaskan native tribes fell into the category of animism. This is a belief that all things in nature are inhabited by spirits. The natives also generally believed that there were good shamans and bad shamans. Disease and misfortune were brought to the native villages by the bad shamans, while good shamans would use their magic to keep the villages safe and protected.

15. The Tlingit and another Alaskan native group, known as the Haida, were known for their totem poles. Nathan Jackson, who is the most famous totem pole carver in the entire world, is based in Alaska. Jackson works at the Saxman Carving Shed, which is located near Ketchikan, Alaska. Tourists can watch him carve totem poles throughout most of the summer.

16. Inuit will not hunt Orcas, otherwise known as killer whales. This is because they believe the spirit of the whale will remember their boat and come back to kill them eventually.

17. The Alaskan natives ate and some still eat narwhal. Narwhal, which is rich in Vitamin C, helped prevent natives from developing scurvy during the times when Vitamin C-rich plants were hard to come by in the state.

18. Anchorage was home to Athabascans before European settlers arrived. The tribe fished, hunted, and lived throughout the region. Today, the city is home to members of other Alaskan native tribes. This is the reason Anchorage is one of the most culturally diverse cities in the United States.

19. Although the Inuit are the most frequently talked about Alaskan native tribe, it might surprise you to learn that they're *not* the Alaskan native group with the highest population today. A 2000 U.S. Census found that there were 16,581 Inuit/Inupiat living throughout the United States. 14,178 of those lived in Alaska. But a 2001 U.S. Census found that there were more than 24,000 Yupik living in the United States, with 22,000 of those residing in Alaska. There are believed to be only a little more than 7,000 Aleut living in Alaska.

20. Alcoholism and suicide are both common problems affecting Alaskan natives in modern times. Alaskan natives have been found to have a higher suicide rate than other Native Americans.

Young Yupik men have been found to be the most at risk of taking their own lives. Alcoholism is also associated with poor health outcomes and violence for Alaska's native groups. It's been estimated that 12% of Alaskan native deaths are caused by alcohol. The rate of fetal-alcohol syndrome is also seven times higher than it is throughout the rest of the country.

Test Yourself – Questions and Answers

1. Today, Alaska's natives account for approximately what percent of the state's current population?

   a. 15%
   b. 20%
   c. 1%

2. Due to its cultural significance, Alaskan natives are the only ones who can legally hunt which of the following bears?

   a. Grizzly bears
   b. Polar bears
   c. Seals

3. When Alaskan natives take part in an "Eskimo kiss," or "kunik," what are they actually doing?

   a. Making out with someone they love
   b. Smelling each other's hair and cheeks
   c. Making each other's noses warm

4. How many Alaskan native languages are spoken in the state today?

   a. 5
   b. 1
   c. 20

5. Alaskan natives generally made their hunting armor from:

   a. Walrus ivory and leather
   b. Walrus ivory and beads
   c. Walrus ivory and seal skin

Answers

1. a.
2. b.
3. b.
4. c.
5. a.

CHAPTER THREE

ALASKA'S POP CULTURE & SPORTS

Have you ever wondered which celebrities and athletes were born or raised in the state of Alaska? Do you know which famous singer was born in the state? Do you know which reality TV shows take place in the state? Hint: there's more than one! Have you ever wondered what the state sport is? What do you know about professional sports teams in Alaska? To find out the answers to these and other random facts about the Last Frontier, read on!

This Musician is From Alaska, and Her Family Has a Reality Show

Today, she's most well-known for her '90s hits "Foolish Games" and "You Were Meant for Me," but did you know that pop/folk singer Jewel was raised in Alaska?

The singer, who has sold over 30 million albums

worldwide, is really named Jewel Kilcher. Jewel lived on a 700-acre homestead in Anchorage with her parents shortly after she was born. After her parents got divorced, she lived with her father in the small town of Homer, Alaska. The home she was raised in didn't have water, indoor plumbing, or heat. They had an outhouse and a coal stove. They lived off fish they caught, cattle they raised, and garden vegetables. Jewel has said that she rode horses every day in the summer and that she loved her Alaskan upbringing.

It was in Alaska that Jewel began performing music. She and her father performed as a father/daughter duo at roadhouses and hotels, such as the Hilton and the Hotel Captain Cook in Anchorage. Jewel also learned how to yodel from her father.

When Jewel was fifteen years old, she worked at a dance studio in Anchorage. The studio's instructor referred her to Interlochen Arts Academy in Michigan, where she received a partial scholarship for the operatic voice program. Her hometown helped her raise the rest of the funds she needed to go to college. Talk about a close-knit community!

It was at the Interlochen Arts Academy that Jewel learned to play the guitar and started songwriting. Once she finished school, she relocated to San Diego. She worked as a barista at Java Joe's in San Diego, which is where she made her debut album.

The rest is history! Her first single "Who Will Save Your Soul" hit No. 11 on the *Billboard* Hot 100 and the singer steadily grew to fame. But there's more…

Did you know Jewel's family have a reality TV show called *Alaska: The Last Frontier*? The show, which is aired on the *Discovery Channel*, features the Kilcher family and extended family on their journeys through farming, hunting, and other pioneering activities in Alaska. Jewel has even appeared on the show a few times.

Alaska: The Last Frontier did face some controversy back in 2015 when Jewel's father Atz, his wife Jane, and a company involved in the show's production broke a law while filming the show. A helicopter was used to make a bear hunt. Spotting prey or otherwise hunting with a helicopter is a crime in Alaska. The charges against the Kilcher family were eventually dropped, but the production company was fined a little over $17,000.

As of 2018, *Alaska: The Last Frontier* has been on the air for seven seasons.

Sarah Palin Also Had a Reality TV Show Based in Alaska

The Kilcher family isn't the only somewhat famous family who has been a part of a reality TV show based in the Last Frontier. Sarah Palin also had a reality TV show of her own, which was called *Sarah Palin's Alaska*.

Sarah Palin's Alaska only ran for one season back in 2010, when it was aired on *TLC*. The show was a combination of documentary and travelogue.

The show received a lot of mixed reviews. Some commended Palin for being brave enough to show the reality TV show side of herself, in spite of her political career. Some felt that the show gave an inaccurate impression of Palin's real life. An author named Nick Jans said the show proved that Sarah Palin didn't know much about Alaska's outdoors, claiming that most of the activities on the show were touristy and guided tours.

The first episode attracted 5 million viewers, with the subsequent episodes averaging about 3 million viewers. While this is a lot of viewers for a *TLC* show, the show wasn't picked up for a second season. It was believed that Sarah Palin didn't want to do a second season because she was preparing for a presidential run in 2012, but she never actually ran for office. Did her plans to run for president fall through or did she have a disagreement with someone at *TLC*? The world may never know.

A Classic American Novel Was Inspired by the Author's Journey Through Alaska

Did you know that one of the most famous classic American novels of all time is not only based on but also inspired by the author's travel to the Last Frontier? Can you guess what book that is? The answer is *The Call of the Wild* by Jack London, who was inspired to write the American classic masterpiece due to his own journey through Alaska.

While Jack London was from California, he traveled to Alaska and Canada during the Klondike Gold Rush. London lived in Canada for a short time, but he passed through the Skagway in Alaska like many others did during the time. It was while he was traveling through the Last Frontier that he got the inspiration behind *The Call of the Wild.*

First, a little background information on the story. *The Call of the Wild* is based on a dog named Buck, who is taken from his home on a ranch in California. Buck is sold as a sled dog in Alaska, where he must survive in the harsh climate. In order to survive, he's forced to dominate other dogs. By the end of the novel, Buck learns to be a leader in the wild.

London's inspiration for the novel came from the dogs that were used in place of horses to transport material over the White Pass, or "Dead Horse Pass." Horses were often found dead because they couldn't survive the steep ascent down the pass at the Skagway.

As for the dog that inspired the main character of the book? Well, that inspiration didn't come from Alaska. Jack London saw many dogs, including a lot of prized Husky sled dogs while he was in Canada, but it was a St. Bernard-Scotch Collie mix that the character of Buck was based on. The dog that inspired London to write the character of Buck belonged to his landlords and friends Marshall Latham Bond and Louis Whitford Bond. There's a photograph of the dog at Beinecke Library at Yale University.

The Call of the Wild may be a classic novel today, but it wasn't that easy for Jack London to get the book published. The story idea was originally turned down due to alleged lack of interest in Alaska. After London had written the novel, it was published by *The Saturday Evening Post* and later by Macmillan in 1903. Since its release, the book has remained in print ever since. To this day, the book is still commonly taught and read in high schools throughout the United States.

A Popular Romantic Comedy Was Set in an Alaska Town, but it Wasn't Actually Filmed in the State

One of the most well-known romantic comedies of the 2000s took place in an Alaska town, but you might be surprised to learn that it wasn't actually filmed in the Last Frontier.

The Proposal, which starred Sandra Bullock and Ryan Reynolds, is set in the town of Sitka, Alaska. The movie features many aspects of Alaska. For example, blackout curtains are used in the movie, which takes place in the summer when the sunlight shines all day and night. The movie also features eagles, which are quite abundant in Alaska with the state's population of 30,000. Ferries and air travel are prominent in the movie.

When you're watching the movie, it's hard to imagine that it could have been filmed anywhere *but* Sitka, Alaska. Unfortunately, if you're a fan of the rom-com, it might disappoint you to learn that the movie was not actually filmed in Sitka. At all. Not even one scene. The movie's real film location was in Rockport. Massachusetts. Areas of Rockport were even temporarily remodeled to resemble Sitka.

Another film that wasn't actually filmed in Alaska, even though it took place in the state? *The Guardian*, starring Ashton Kutcher and Kevin Costner. The scenes that took place in Alaska were actually filmed at the CG Air Station in Elizabeth City, North Carolina.

But Lots of Other Movies Have Been Filmed in Alaska

While *The Proposal* and *The Guardian* weren't filmed in Alaska, other movies have been. With its beautiful (and, at times, creepy) scenery, Alaska has been a popular place for movies to be filmed. Some of the most well-known movies that have been filmed in the state include:

- *Star Trek VI: The Undiscovered Country* – You might be surprised to learn that this *Star Trek* movie was filmed at the Knik Glacier and in Chugach State Park.
- *The Thing* – This horror movie, which was all the rage when it came out in 1982, is about a research station in Alaska being infiltrated by an extraterrestrial/parasitic-like thing. The movie was filmed in Juneau, Alaska.
- *Insomnia* – This movie, which starred Al Pacino, Robin Williams, and Hilary Swank was about two Los Angeles detectives who investigate a murder in an Alaskan town. The movie is set in winter, so it's dark the whole time in the movie, which was primarily filmed in Valdez and Hyder, Alaska.
- *White Fang* – The 1991 movie based on Jack London's novel of the same name was filmed throughout Alaska.

A Movie Based on a True Story Was Also Filmed in Alaska

Did you know that a movie that was based on a true story was filmed in Alaska?

The 2007 film *Into the Wild* is one of the most well-known movies to ever be set and filmed in Alaska. Some of the places where the film was set include Denali National Park and Anchorage, Healy, and Cantwell, Alaska. You may or may not know that the movie, which was directed by Sean Penn, is based on a book of the same name. What you also might not know is that the Jon Krakauer's book *Into the Wild* is nonfiction.

Both the book and the film are based on the "real life" story of Christopher McCandless, a hiker who was known as "Alexander Supertramp." He traveled across North America before hitchhiking to Alaska in 1992. He traveled the Stampede Trail, with few supplies and plans to live off the land. His decomposing body was later found by a hunter along the trail. McCandless's body was found in a bus that had been converted into a shelter, which he had been living in prior to his death.

The circumstances behind McCandless's death have been highly debated. In his book *Into the Wild*, author Jon Krakauer poses the theory that McCandless died due to "rabbit starvation," which happens when someone relies on lean game for nutrition. Krakauer also thinks that McCandless may have died due to eating seeds that are toxic to humans. This theory has been a controversial one, however, as scientific analysis of the seeds found no toxins that could have contributed to Christopher McCandless's death.

The bus McCandless used as shelter is infamous among hikers today. The bus, which has been nicknamed "The Magic Bus," can still be found along the Stampede Trail today. There's a plaque honoring Christopher McCandless inside the bus.

A Disney Voice Actress is From Alaska

Did you know the actress behind the voice of the main character in Disney's animated film *Pocahontas* is from Alaska?

Actress Irene Bedard was born in Anchorage, Alaska. The actress's background is made up of Inuit, Yupik, Inupiat, Cree, and Métis ancestry. In addition to being the voice behind Pocahontas, Bedard was also used as the physical model for the movie's animators who illustrated Pocahontas. This has been somewhat of a controversial issue, as Pocahontas wasn't actually an Alaskan native.

Nevertheless, Irene Bedard has been a great role model for Native American talent throughout the country.

In 1995, Irene Bedard was even chosen as one of *People* magazine's "50 Most Beautiful People."

Bedard has had roles in a number of movies and made for TV series about Native Americans. She played in the 2005 movie *The New World*, but this time she played Pocahontas's mother rather than Pocahontas herself. The same year, she also played in the mini-series *Into the West*, in which she played a half-Lakota, half-white Margaret "Light Shines" Wheeler.

Irene Bedard's resume even extends beyond movies and TV. In 2017, she also played in Jay-Z's music video for his song "Family Feud."

Rapper Pitbull Once Made a Trip to Alaska All Because of a Prank

If you're going to prank a rapper, why not send him to one of the most remote locations in the United States? At least, that's what David Thorpe must have been thinking when he played a really... well, *unique* prank on rapper Pitbull.

It happened back in 2012 when Pitbull took part in a contest to advertise Sheets Energy Strips. The contest rules were simple enough: Pitbull would visit the Walmart that received the most Facebook "likes" from fans. How could this have gone wrong?

Well, it did. It went very wrong.

David Thorpe, who was a writer for the (now-defunct) newspaper the *Boston Phoenix* at the time, started a prank. He encouraged his followers to vote on the most remote Walmart in the entire country. It turns out that this Walmart is located in Kodiak, Alaska, a town where there's only a population of 6,000 people.

One might think that Pitbull would back out on his promise to visit the Walmart, but he didn't. Pitbull held true to his word and ended up going to Kodiak, Alaska, but in a surprise twist, he invited David Thorpe to go with him! Yeah, that's right. The guy who started this prank ended up going to state, too. (Who was really the victim in this prank?).

Not only did Pitbull perform for a crowd of hundreds at the Coast Guard base in Kodiak, but he even got a gift during his visit: a Walmart care package, which included bear repellant. Makes you wonder if he ever ended up using it.

One Alaska-Based Documentary Show Airs in More Than 200 Countries

The documentary TV show, *Deadliest Catch*, airs on the *Discovery Channel* and in more than 200 countries throughout the world!

The show depicts true events related to Alaskan king crab, opilio crab, and bairdi crab fishing. The fishing fleet in the show is based at Dutch Harbor in the Aleutian Islands.

The name of the show comes from the dangerous and

even potentially deadly nature of this line of work. Many may not know this, but commercial fishing is considered to be one of the deadliest jobs in the United States.

As of 2017, the show had aired its 13th season.

Curt Schilling Was Born in Alaska

Did you know that famous Major League Baseball (MLB) player Curt Schilling is from Anchorage, Alaska?

Schilling is one of only eleven Alaskan-born baseball players to ever make it to the MLB.

Curt Schilling played for several teams in the MLB. It was under his leadership that the Philadelphia Phillies won the World Series back in 1993. He won championships when he played for the Arizona Diamondbacks in 2001 and the Boston Red Sox in 2004 and 2007.

Despite his birthplace, Curt Schilling considers Pittsburgh to be his home.

NFL Player Scott Gomez is From Alaska

If you follow hockey, you might be interested to know that Scott Gomez was only the 5th Alaskan to ever play in the National Hockey League (NHL).

Gomez, who was born in Anchorage, originally played for the Alaska Aces. He later went on to play for the Tri-City Americans of the Western Hockey League when he was drafted by the New Jersey Devils. He led the New Jersey Devils to win the Stanley Cup in the 2000 playoffs.

Gomez later went to play for several other teams in the league: the New York Rangers, Montreal Canadians, San Jose Sharks, Florida Panthers, St. Louis Blues, and the Ottawa Senators.

And to think it all started in Alaska!

Dog Mushing is the Official State Sport

While it might not be what you think of when sports come to mind, the official state sport of Alaska is dog mushing. The state sport was established in 1972.

The state sport is deeply rooted in Alaska history. As you may remember from earlier chapters, sled dogs were originally used as a form of transportation throughout Alaska, like when Balto and Togo carried medicine. Originally started by the Alaskan natives to get to locations where they could go hunting, using sled dogs as a means of transportation eventually evolved into sled dog racing.

Today, dog mushing is a sport that's enjoyed at both the professional and recreational levels in Alaska.

Many of Alaska's residents have two or more dogs that they keep for recreational dog mushing. Mushing is something that people take part in throughout the entire year in Alaska. During the summer months, mushers work on training and exercising their dogs. They use sleds with wheels. This helps keep the dogs in shape for the winter season.

Sled dogs are generally kept in what's known as a "dog lot," or a dog yard that looks like a mini dog village. Each dog has its own house, and the dog houses line the streets. Straw is used to insulate the dog houses in winter, which helps keep the dogs warm during even the coldest months. During the summer months, the houses provide the dogs with shade.

At a professional level, there are a few major dog mushing races that take place in the state each year.

The Largest Dog Sled Race in the World is Held in Alaska

Unsurprisingly, the largest dog sled race in the world is held in Alaska. The Iditarod Trail Sled Dog Race is held in Alaska every year during the month of March. Known as "The Last Great Race," the Iditarod is a 1,000-mile race that spans from Anchorage to Nome, Alaska.

Since it started back in 1973, the Iditarod Trail Sled Dog Race has taken dog mushers anywhere between eight and twenty days or longer to complete the race. Dog mushers from 14 different countries have competed in the Iditarod.

Some of the records that have been set during the Iditarod Trail Sled Dog Race have been set by the following:

- Dick Wilmarth, who was the first winner of the race. Wilmarth completed the race in 20 days, 0 hours, 49 minutes, and 41 seconds.
- Rick Swenson, who became the first to win four races in 1982. He's the only dog musher who has ever won the race during three different decades.
- Mary Shields, who was the first woman to complete the race in 1974.
- Libby Riddles, who became the first woman to ever win the race in 1985. It's worth noting that she was the only one who competed in the race that year due to a blizzard.
- Doug Swingley, who was the first non-Alaskan to ever win the race in 1995. Swingley was from Montana.
- Mitch Seavey, who held the fastest record as of 2017. Seavey completed the race in 8 days, 3 hours, 40 minutes, and 13 seconds.

The Iditarod Trail Sled Dog Race plays an important role in Alaska's culture. Winners of the race are viewed as local celebrities.

The Iditarod is also not the only race that's held every

year in Alaska. The 1,000-mile Yukon Quest International Sled Dog Race also takes place in the state. The race is the biggest long-distance race in the world. The race takes place every February and runs from Whitehorse, Canada to Fairbanks, Alaska. The race started out running from Canada to Alaska early on, but it typically changes directions every year. Due to its rugged terrain and long distances in between checkpoints, the 1,000-mile Yukon Quest International has been called "the toughest race on earth."

There are two other dog mushing competitions which are held in Fairbanks. The Limited North American Championship, which is a three-day event that consists of sprint sled dog and skijoring races. (Skijoring is when sled dogs pull skiers). The event takes place in March.

The Open North American Championship, which also takes place in March, is the oldest sled dog race that continues to run. Another three-day event, the races begin and end in downtown Fairbanks. The race is said to draw in some of the world's fastest dog mushers.

Alaska Has No Professional Sports Teams

Can you name an Alaskan professional sports team? No? It may (or may not) surprise you to learn that Alaska has *no* professional sports teams. Zero. None. Not even one.

If you're an avid sports fan, a state without even a single professional sports team might seem crazy to you. You might be wondering why this is. Well, there are said to be several reasons.

One of the main reasons is because Alaska's low population wouldn't be conductive to professional sports game audiences. For comparison's sake: the population of Anchorage is around 300,000, while Houston, Texas has a population of 2.3 million. The number of stadium seats at Dallas Cowboys Stadium alone is 100,000—which is one-third of Anchorage's total population! The odds of selling out an entire arena for a sporting event in Alaska seem unlikely.

Another one of the reasons why Alaska doesn't have any sports teams is because of transportation reasons. It's simply not logical. It would be too costly for teams to travel to Alaska or for an Alaskan team to travel throughout the continental U.S.

There's also the issue of Alaska's climate conditions. Not only isn't the climate well-suited for teams to train, but it's also not ideal for teams to play.

That being said, sports fans don't have to be completely let down by the Last Frontier. The good news is that there are several minor league sports teams in the state. There are two minor league baseball teams: The Anchorage Bucs and the Anchorage Glacier Pilots. There's also a minor league hockey team, the Alaska Aces.

Alaska is also home to college sports as well through the University of Alaska Anchorage. The sports teams affiliated with the university include both men's and women's basketball, men's and women's cross country, men's and women's track and field, men's ice hockey, women's gymnastics, women's volleyball, and co-ed skiing.

Every year, the Great Alaska Shootout also takes place in the state. This is a college basketball tournament that's held on Thanksgiving at the University of Alaska Anchorage. Several teams throughout the U.S. go there for the tournament.

Alaska Has Tried to Host the Olympics More Than Once

Did you know that Alaska has tried to host the Olympics on more than one occasion? Anchorage was chosen as the United State candidate to host the Olympic Games in both 1992 and 1994. Sadly, the state wasn't chosen either of those times.

It has been rumored that Anchorage is going to consider bidding to host the Olympic Games in 2026. Will they actually be chosen this time around? Only time will tell!

RANDOM FACTS

1. Actor Joshua Morrow, who plays Nicholas Newman on *The Young and the Restless,* was born in Juneau. His character is a heartthrob favorite among fans of the show, and Morrow has earned an Emmy award for the role. Morrow has been a member of the show's cast since 1994.

2. Actor Nathan West is an Anchorage native. He attended Service High School in Anchorage before going on to play Mary's friends Johnny in *7th Heaven* with his now wife, Chyler Leigh, who played Frankie. After *7th Heaven*, Nathan West went on to play in the movies *Bring It On* and *Not Another Teen Movie*.

3. Today, Wikipedia is a popular household name. Whether you love or hate it, you know the online encyclopedia exists. Did you know that the website's co-founder, Larry Sanger, grew up in Anchorage? His family moved to the city when he was seven years old.

4. Author Robin Hobb, whose real name is Margaret Astrid Lindholm Ogden, was raised in Fairbanks from the age of 10. Her books have sold more than one million copies and include the *Farseer Trilogy* (*Assassin's Apprentice*, *Royal Assassin*, and

Assassin's Quest), and the spinoff *Tawny Man Trilogy* (*Fool's Errand*, *The Golden Fool*, and *Fool's Fate*).

5. Charles Wood, who starred on Broadway in the 1940s and 1950s, grew up in Iditarod, Alaska. Wood's most notable performances were as Hortensio in *Kiss Me, Kate*, which won five Tony Awards and as Morrie in *Wish You Were Here*, during which he starred alongside Jack Cassidy and Florence Henderson, who was just a newcomer at the time.

6. Musical festivals play an important role in local Alaska culture. The Alaska Folk Festival, which is held every April in Juneau, is the state's most popular music festival. Some of the other most well-known music festivals in the state include the Anchorage Folk Festival and the Athabascan Old-Time Fiddling Festival.

7. Former Playboy Bunny Holly Madison spent part of her childhood in Craig, Alaska, which is located on Prince of Wales Island. They moved to the state when Madison was just two years old and left when she was in middle school. Most known for her seven-year relationship with Hugh Hefner, Madison was also featured in the *E! Network* show *The Girls Next Door*.

8. Actor James Morrison was raised in Anchorage, Alaska. Morrison is best-known for his role as

Bill Buchanan in *24*. Some other small but noteworthy roles Morrison has had include as Gordon Murphy in *Revenge*, CIA Senator Phillips in *NCIS*, Gray Campbell in *Law & Order: LA*, Jerome Jensen in *Suits*, Warner Vander Hoek in *The Mentalist*, and William White in *Private Practice*.

9. An Anchorage-based reality TV show called "Mounted in Alaska," which aired on the *History Channel*, was a one of a kind show. It was based on Knight's Taxidermy and their journeys in the business.

10. *The Alaskan Bush People* is a reality TV show that's filmed on location in the Hoonah, Alaska area and Chichagof Island. The show follows the Brown family as they travel Alaska in order to build temporary shelters and then as they build a homestead on Chichagof Island. There has been a lot of controversy about the legitimacy of the show, which airs on the *Discovery Channel*. Some have questioned if the show is actually "reality," with people accusing Billy Brown of being from Texas and not from Alaska. The Brown family denies these claims as being true, however. After writing his book, *One Wave at a Time*, Brown allegedly moved his family to the continental United States in order to sell the story. A production crew followed the Browns when they

moved back to Alaska, where the family recreated the lifestyle Brown talks about in his book.

11. Artis the Spoonman, known as just "Spoonman" for short, is a street performer based in Seattle, Washington. Spoonman, who uses spoons to make music, is from Kodiak, Alaska.

12. A number of songs have been written about Alaska. Some of these include "When It's Springtime in Alaska" by Johnny Horton, "North to Alaska" by Jerry Lee Lewis, and "Talkin' Goin' to Alaska Blues" by Shawn Mullins. John Denver has also recorded more than one song about Alaska. Denver's songs about the Last Frontier include "Postcard from Paris," "Alaska & Me," and "American Child."

13. Author Dana Stabenow is from Anchorage, Alaska. Many of the crime/mystery and suspense/thriller author's novels are set in the state.

14. Sarah Palin's daughter, Bristol, had a documentary TV show that aired on *Lifetime* called *Bristol Palin: Life's a Tripp*. The show followed Bristol Palin, who was then new teen mother of Tripp, as she relocated to Los Angeles from Alaska and then back to Alaska. Bristol Palin also made an appearance on the show *Dancing with the Stars*. Though Palin didn't win on *DWTS*,

she did make it to third place on the show.

15. The first season of the *Discovery Channel*'s reality TV show *Gold Rush* takes place in Alaska. It features six guys from Oregon who head to Porcupine Creek, Alaska in search of gold. The people on the show know nothing about gold mining and have to learn how to do it. If you have an interest in gold mining or panning yourself, this show just might be for you.

16. In 2018, a record-breaking number of Alaskan athletes competed in the Olympic Games. U.S. Ski and Snowboard contestants included siblings Reese Hanneman and Logan Hanneman of Fairbanks, and Tyler Kornfield, Rosie Frankowski, Caitlin Patterson, and Scott Patterson of Anchorage. Kikkan Randall, Rosie Brennan, Sadie Bjornsen, and Erik Bjornsen of Anchorage also competed in skiing. Half of the Nordic team was from Alaska.

17. The first women's roller derby team in Anchorage was formed by a group of women in 2007 after watching roller derby throughout the United States. The roller derby team is called the Rag City Rollergirls.

18. Former NBA player Trajan Langdon was the first Alaskan to ever play for the National Basketball Association. Trajan Langdon was raised in

Anchorage, Alaska. He played basketball for East Anchorage High School and led the team to the 1994 state championship. He later went on to play basketball for Duke University. At one point, he held the record for the highest number of 3-point field goals and earned the nickname of "The Alaskan Assassin." Langdon was drafted by the NBA's the Cleveland Cavaliers.

19. Former NBA star Carlos Boozer grew up in Juneau, Alaska. He would practice outside his middle school with his dad, even during the harsh Alaskan winters. After leading his high school team, the Juneau-Douglas Bears to two state titles, he was recruited by a number of college basketball teams. He decided to play for Duke University and helped the team win the 2001 NCAA championship. He was later drafted to the NBA and played for the Cleveland Cavaliers. Boozer later played for the Chicago Bulls and Los Angeles Lakers.

20. Alaskan native Walter Harper was a mountain climber who was the first to ever reach the top of Mount McKinley in June of 1913.

Test Yourself – Questions and Answers

1. Where did the singer Jewel grow up?

   a. Homer, Alaska
   b. Juneau, Alaska
   c. Nome, Alaska

2. Which musician went to Alaska because of a prank?

   a. Usher
   b. Pitbull
   c. Justin Timberlake

3. Which American classic novel was inspired by the Klondike Gold Rush in Alaska and the Yukon?

   a. *To Kill a Mockingbird*
   b. *The Call of the Wild*
   c. *The Great Gatsby*

4. Which show is *not* filmed in Alaska?

   a. *Alaska: The Last Frontier*
   b. *Deadliest Catch*
   c. *Survivor*

5. The first woman to win the Iditarod Trail Sled Dog Race was:

   a. Sarah Palin
   b. Mary Shields
   c. Libby Riddles

Answers

1. a.
2. b.
3. b.
4. c.
5. c.

CHAPTER FOUR

FACTS ABOUT ALASKA'S ATTRACTIONS

If you're thinking about planning a trip to Alaska, you probably already know that the state is a popular destination among nature lovers. With eight national parks, Alaska has the second highest number of national parks in the country—second only to California. This makes it just about any nature lover's dream come true.

But how much do you *really* know about the state's attractions? Do you know which marine animal can only be seen at certain time of the year? Do you know what Alaskan attraction came to exist as the result of a prize? To find out the answers to these questions and read other facts about Alaska's attractions, read on!

The Largest National Park in the United States is in Alaska

Did you know that Alaska is home to the largest national park in America? Wrangell-St. Elias National Park encompasses 13,188,00 acres, making it *six times* the size of Yellowstone National Park and larger than nine U.S. states.

Four different major mountain ranges can be found within the park, which includes the St. Elias, the Wrangells, the Alaska, and the Chugach ranges. As a result, nine of the tallest mountain peaks in the United States can be found within Wrangell-St. Elias National Park.

More than 150 glaciers can also be found within the park's boundaries, including the Malaspina. The Malaspina, which is larger than the state of Rhode Island, is the largest piedmont glacier in all of North America. Hubbard Glacier, which is the largest tidewater glacier in Alaska, is also located in Wrangell-St. Elias. Nabesna Glacier, which can be found in the park, is the longest valley glacier in the world.

More than 9,000,000 acres of Wrangell-St. Elias National Park has earned it the title of the "single largest wilderness in the United States."

The national park is also home to volcanoes. Mount Wrangell itself is an active volcano, and Mount

Churchill in the St. Elias mountain range has exploded within the past 2,000 years.

But It's Not the Most Visited National Park in the State!

It may surprise you to learn that while Wrangell-St. Elias National Park is geographically the largest national park and home to some of the most beautiful natural wonders in the country, it's *not* the most visited national park in Alaska. In fact, Wrangell-St. Elias National Park only saw 68,292 visitors in 2017. So, what is the state's most visited national park?

That title would go to Denali National Park, which saw 642,809 visitors in 2017. Denali National Park is also the No. 1 most popular tourist attraction in all of Alaska.

The national park encompasses more than 6,000,000 acres. The park's landscape consists of forest, tundra, rock, snow, and glaciers, with the longest glacier in the park being the Kahiltna Glacier. At the center of the park is a mountain, which you might recognize by a different name: Mt. McKinley.

Mt. McKinley Has Been Renamed

There's no doubt that you've heard of Mt. McKinley. But did you know there's no longer a mountain with that name? Here's why.

Denali was once known as Mt. McKinley. Back in the late 1890s, a guy named William Dickey named the mountain Mt. McKinley in honor of the presidential candidate at the time, William McKinley. Dickey, who was a gold prospector, allegedly chose the name because McKinley was a supporter of the Klondike Gold Rush. This decision was frowned upon by some because the-then presidential candidate, future president had never even set foot in Alaska.

Because of the mountain's name, that meant that Denali National Park was also once known as Mt. McKinley National Park as well.

The name was always a controversial subject among the locals from the get-go. The locals had always referred to the mountain as Denali. The word had originated from the Koyukon Athabaskans, who called the mountain's peak Denali, which means "the high one" or "the tall one." The Athabaskan natives had been calling the mountain Denali for centuries before the name "Mt. McKinley" was chosen. So, needless to say, most of the locals continued to call the mountain Denali, the name they had always known it as.

In 1975, the Alaska Board of Geographic Names changed the name to Denali on the state level. They requested to have the name changed on the federal level, too, but the request was blocked by Congress. The U.S. Board on Geographic Names continued to call it Mt. McKinley until President Obama's administration changed the mountain's name back to Denali in 2015.

People Die Trying to Climb Denali, But People Continue to Try

Denali is the highest mountain peak in the United States, and in all of North America. Its peak is more than 20,000 feet above sea level. In addition, Denali is the third highest of the Seven Summits or the highest peaks of the seven continents. The only mountains that are higher are Mount Everest and Aconcagua.

If you've ever thought about climbing the mountain, you may be wondering what the likelihood of actually reaching the top is. Among the estimated 32,000 people who have tried, only about half have actually succeeded.

Climbing the mountain also isn't for the fainthearted. It may or may not surprise you to learn that people die every year when they attempt to climb Denali. It has been estimated that approximately 1,200 people try to climb Denali each year and that one out of every 200 people dies trying. Given these estimates, about six people die every year when they attempt to climb the mountain. Park rangers and volunteers end up saving many more, however.

Are you willing to brave it?

If you're thinking about trying to climb Denali, it's important to be prepared. In order to climb the mountain, you must obtain a permit. You should apply for the permit 60 days ahead of time. There are also fees involved with climbing the mountain.

Due to weather conditions, the best time to climb the mountain is between May and July. Temperatures tend to be -30 to -70 degrees Fahrenheit between November and April, with temperatures even on the lower side in early May. Going too late in the season means you won't be able to get picked up by plane since they can't land on exposed glaciers. Instead, you would need to walk for 10 days through the forest.

It's also worth noting that it takes most people one to two weeks to become acclimated to any given altitude on Denali. You also lose your acclimation within a few weeks. It has been recommended that you limit your ascent to 300 meters, or 1,000 feet, each day you climb the mountain. Be sure to do your research ahead of time to make sure you're allowing yourself enough time to complete the climb.

Climbing Denali isn't recommended for inexperienced hikers. It's only best suited for seasoned hikers.

Humpback Whales Can Be Seen at Glacier Bay National Park, But Only Seasonally

Glacier Bay National Park is home to various types of wildlife. Mountain goats roam the cliffs, moose hang out in the brush, and sea lions, sea otters, and harbor seals can be found among the water and coastlines. Both Grizzly bears (also known as brown bears) and black bears are frequently spotted at the national park. Black bears occupy the forested areas of the park, while Grizzly bears can be spotted in all areas of the park.

In terms of wildlife, one of Glacier Bay National Park's biggest draws is its humpback whales. Humpback whales, which are endangered, span 40 to 50 feet long and generally weigh more than 35 tons. Something you might not know about the park's whales is that they can only be seen seasonally. They generally migrate to Hawaii during the winter where they mate and give birth. The 2,500-mile trip takes the whales a month to complete.

While they're in Hawaii, humpback whales don't eat. When they return to Alaska for spring, summer, and fall, they fill up on high-calorie fish, like herring and capelin to sustain themselves through the winter.

Fortunately, most tourists visit the state during the summer months, so you might be able to catch a glimpse of humpback whales at Glacier Bay National

Park. If you're a humpback whale or marine animal lover, this is one attraction you won't want to miss out on if you ever visit Alaska!

You Can Take a Polar Bear Expedition in Alaska

Have you ever wanted to see a polar bear up close and personal? If you've ever dreamt of seeing a polar bear in the wild, then you're in luck. The Northern Alaska Tour Company has a polar bear expedition that allows you to do exactly that.

When the expedition begins, you'll travel on a 9-passenger Piper Chieftain aircraft that will take you above some remote locations throughout Alaska. While you're in the air, you may be able to catch a glimpse of polar bears and herds of caribou from above.

After you land in Kaktovik, you'll travel on open-air boats that fit 6 passengers. They'll be driven by U.S. Coast Guard certified captains, who will take you to the barrier islands. It's there where you'll really get the chance to see polar bears, as they like to hang out on the barrier islands during the daytime. You'll be most likely to spot polar bears at the "bone pile," which is where they go to find old whale bones to chew.

If you ever have the chance to visit Alaska, this is one tourist attraction you won't want to miss out on!

The Alaska Zoo Started Out Because of a Contest

The Alaska Zoo is one of Anchorage's most popular attractions, drawing in nearly 200,000 visitors a year. Today, the zoo is home to animals that are native to Alaska, as well as some exotic animals, such as tigers, camels, and yaks. But did you know that the zoo started out with just *one* animal, all thanks to a contest? It may sound strange, but let's start from the beginning.

In 1966, an Anchorage grocer named Jack Snyder won a Chiffon toilet paper contest, which offered a prize of either $3,000 or a baby elephant. Snyder opted for the elephant, which surprised the company, who hadn't expected anyone to choose that prize option. The company searched for an elephant, who turned out to be an 18-month baby Asian elephant named Annabelle. Annabelle had originally been a circus elephant.

During her first summer in Alaska, Annabelle toured the state. Alaskans grew to love her. Who wouldn't love a baby elephant, after all?

When winter came, Snyder had to find a place to house Annabelle. He ended up deciding on the Diamond H Horse Ranch in Anchorage, which was the only place around that offered heated stables. The ranch was owned by Sammye Seawell.

After three months of feeding the baby elephant, Jack Snyder decided to give her Sammye Seawell.

As people began to take an interest in Annabelle, Seawell started a non-profit corporation with the goal of building a place where people could go to see and learn about animals. In 1969, the Alaska Children's Zoo opened. It featured Annabelle and other animals that had been donated to the zoo, which was located adjacent to the Diamond H Horse Ranch.

In 1980, the name of the zoo was changed to the Alaska Zoo. Three years later, the zoo acquired a female African elephant named Maggie, who became Annabelle's companion.

When Annabelle's trainers put a paintbrush in her trunk in 1991, something truly magical happened. The elephant began to splatter brushstrokes on canvasses. The elephant could paint! Annabelle began to create artwork in front of the zoo's visitors, making her even more of an attraction among zoo goers. People even began to buy Annabelle's artwork.

Annabelle died in 1997 at 33 years old following a foot infection. Her death left Maggie lonely. Despite some controversy, the zoo decided to keep Maggie alone before eventually sending her to PAWS sanctuary in California in 2007.

It's hard to believe it all started out because of Jack

Snyder's entry in that contest! It's hard to imagine what would have happened if he had chosen the $3,000 for his prize instead.

Alaska Has a Temperate Rain Forest

Alaska might not be the first state that comes to mind when you think of temperate rain forests, but Tongass National Forest is just that.

With its location on Prince of Wales Island, Tongass National Forest is the largest national forest in the United States. It's also one of the most ecologically diverse, with large populations of black bears, wolves, moose, eagles, and various other types of birds. Approximately 25% of the United States' wild-caught salmon comes from Tongass National Forest.

Tongass National Forest takes up 16.8 million acres of land. In spite of its name, about 40% of that is made up of wetlands, snow, ice, rock, and non-forest area, while only 10 million acres is actual forest.

The forest sees an average of one million visitors each year. There are 15 campgrounds across the forest, offering tourists a place to stay with great views of glaciers and bald eagles. There's also an elevated bear-viewing platform in Hyder, Alaska, where you can safely watch both grizzly bears and black bears.

The Northern Lights Can Be Seen Most of the Year in Fairbanks

The aurora borealis, or northern lights, are one of Alaska's most popular tourist draws. With their green, purple, and red lights, the glow that's cast in the sky is caused by charged protons and electrons as they enter the atmosphere.

Fairbanks, Alaska is considered to be one of the best spots to see the aurora borealis. Every year, the city draws in tourists who have made seeing the northern lights an item on their bucket lists.

If you've ever wanted to see the aurora borealis, the good news is that they can be viewed in Alaska for the majority of the year. In fact, they can be seen in the state for about eight out of twelve months. It's been estimated that you can see the northern lights in Fairbanks an average of 243 days a year.

The bad news? The northern lights can't be seen during much of the summer, which is prime tourist season in Alaska. This is because the lights can only be seen when it's dark out. The sky also needs to be clear enough for them to be seen.

If you're planning a trip to Alaska to see the northern lights, they become visible towards the middle to end of August.

Kenai Fjords National Park is Every Bird Lover's Dream

If you love birds, then Kenai Fjords National Park just might be for you.

Spanning across 699,983 acres of land, Kenai Fjords is Alaska's smallest national park. Its unique name comes from two very different cultures. Kenai comes from the Athabaskan natives that resided in the area, while Fjords means "long, glacier-carved inlet" in Old Norse.

There is no doubt that Kenai Fjords National Park is most well-known for its Harding Icefield, where you'll find more than 700 acres of ice that can be up to a mile thick. The Harding Icefield feeds three glaciers. For nature lovers, however, the park's wildlife is its real draw. Mountain goats, coyotes, wolverines, black bears, and moose can be found roaming the area.

But did you know that Kenai Fjords National Park is also a birdwatching hotspot? Bald eagles, peregrine falcons, and tens of thousands of seabirds can be spotted at the park every year. People also go to the park to see puffins, as two different species—tufted puffins and horned puffins—can both be found at Kenai Fjords.

One Alaskan National Park is Home to the World's Largest Grizzly Bear Population

You probably already know that Alaska has a huge bear population. In fact, it's been estimated that there's approximately one bear for every 21 people who live in Alaska. We can all agree that's *a lot* of bears. What you might not have known, however, is that one of Alaska's national parks is home to the largest population of grizzly bears in the entire world.

Katmai National Park is most well-known for its active volcanoes, but the park also has both the largest population of grizzly bears in the world and the largest population of protected grizzly bears in North America. There are approximately 2,000 Grizzly bears who call the 3,922,000-acre park home.

This might seem scary if you're planning a visit to Katmai National Park, but don't worry. Park rangers go to extreme measures to make sure the grizzly bears don't come into contact with humans or their food. In fact, the grizzly bears are basically trained to not pay attention to humans to the point where they aren't even interested in the park's human visitors.

A lot of people tend to get great photos of the grizzly bears when they go salmon fishing in the rivers. The Grizzlies tend to do most of their fishing in July, making this the most ideal time for tourists to visit the park.

The Least Visited National Park in the Country is in Alaska

Did you know the least visited national park in the United States is located in Alaska?

Gates of the Arctic National Park sees only about 10,000 visitors a year. You might think it's because there's not much to see at the park, but that's not the reason the park doesn't see many visitors. The reality is that the park isn't easily accessible to visitors. There are no trails or roads that lead into the park. The only way you can get into Gates of the Arctic is by hiking in or hiring an air taxi. That being said, there are plenty of great reasons to visit the park.

Made up of 8.4 million acres, Gates of the Arctic National Park is the second largest national park in the country. It's geographically larger than the states of Rhode Island and Massachusetts combined, as well as slightly larger than Belgium. It's also the most northern national park in the country.

Gates of the Arctic National Park contains most of the Brooks Range and includes mountains such as Mount Igikpak and Arrigetch Peaks. The park is also home to six rivers, including the 110-mile Kobuk River. The park lays at the continental divide, which separates the drainages from the Arctic Ocean and the Pacific Ocean.

There are a number of Alaskan native tribes that live

within the park, including the Noatak and Kobuk river tribes and the Koyoukan Indians. They live off the herds of caribou that roam the park. Some of the other animals you can expect to see at this park include polar bears, foxes, black bears, bald eagles, coyotes, wolves, peregrine falcons, river otters, moose, coyotes, and more. Camping is permitted within the park.

Portage Glacier is a Huge Alaskan Tourist Attraction

Did you know that Portage Glacier is Alaska's second most visited tourist attraction?

The glacier, which is still active from the Ice Age, is located within Chugach National Forest. Today, the glacier spans across six miles, but it once extended for 14 miles. The glacial receding is what caused the Portage Lake to form.

Although the glacier has been fairly stable since the 1900s, scientists believe that it could eventually melt more in the future thanks to global warming.

Something that most tourists find intriguing about the glacier is the Alaskan ice worm, which can be seen at Portage Glacier (as well as other glaciers throughout Alaska). The ice worm, which resembles earthworms, lives inside of the glacier. It exists on the glacier's pollen and algae. The worms thrive under freezing conditions. Once summer comes and temperatures hit above 40 degrees Fahrenheit, the worm melts and dies.

Alaska SeaLife Center is More Than Just an Aquarium

Alaska SeaLife Center is more than just a public aquarium. It's the only marine mammal rescue and rehabilitation facility in the state.

At its location in Seward, the SeaLife Center opened in May of 1998. In addition to rescue and rehabilitation, the facility focuses on research and conservation. The project cost $55 million, with the majority of funds coming from the Exxon Valdez oil spill settlement.

The SeaLife Center specializes in both marine mammals and seabirds that are found in Alaska. It studies and conserves Stellar sea lions, harbor seals, sea otters, fur seals, and other mammals that live in the state. You can also see fish and birds, including puffins, at the center. The Alaska SeaLife Center allows visitors to have encounters and other experiences with its animals.

There's a Museum to Help You Learn About the Culture of Alaska's Natives

If you're thinking of planning a trip to Alaska, chances are you have an interest in "Eskimo" culture and wish to learn more about it. Well, you're in luck.

The Alaska Native Heritage Center in Anchorage is a museum and cultural center that's designed to help people gain a better understanding of Alaska's native groups. It's an experience unlike any other. The museum features a number of neat things to help tourists learn more about the Alaskan native way of life.

At the center's Gathering Place, you'll get to experience Alaskan native dancing, games, and storytelling.

The Hall of Culture features exhibits focusing on the five main native groups, as well as artwork. Children will have Alaskan native craft opportunities.

The Theatre features films, such as the center's own film, "Stories Given, Stories Shared."

Outside the center, you'll find authentic dwellings Alaska's natives lived in, and you'll learn more about the native way of life.

RANDOM FACTS

1. Beluga Point, which is located just south of Anchorage, is a beluga whale sighting hotspot from mid-July to August. Since 2000, it's been estimated that there are between 300 and 375 living in the area. Orcas can also be seen in the area, as they tend to prey on beluga whales.

2. Six Mile Creek is a 12-mile waterway that was once a popular gold mining spot in Alaska. Today, Six Mile Creek is one of the most popular places in the state to go white water rafting.

3. Iliamna Lake is Alaska's largest lake and the third largest lake in the United States. It's also one of the few places in the entire world where you'll find freshwater seals.

4. The Chugach National Forest has the largest bald eagle population of any of the 48 continental U.S. states combined. At any given time, between 3,000 and 5,000 bald eagles call the forest home.

5. The Arctic National Wildlife Refuge is the largest National Wildlife Refuge in the United States. Some of the wildlife you can expect to find at the refuge include polar bears, wolves, caribou, and bald eagles.

6. Flattop Mountain, which is located within Chugach State Park, is the most climbed mountain in the state of Alaska. The mountain is popular due to its beautiful views of Anchorage and Denali, which can be seen on clear days.

7. Anchorage Museum has a number of Alaskan-themed exhibits, including "Living Our Cultures, Sharing Our Heritage: The First Peoples of Alaska."

8. Denali National Park is home to the wood frog. The park's only amphibian has an interesting rate of survival. Wood frogs freeze during the winter months. Their hearts stop and their lungs stop breathing… but only until springtime comes and they thaw back to life.

9. Chugach State Park spans across 495,000 acres of land, making it one of the four largest state parks in the entire United States.

10. Earthquake Park in Anchorage honors the 1964 earthquake. The 134-acre park is situated in the woods where an entire neighborhood slid into the ocean during the state's devastating earthquake. The park is a popular spot for biking, walking, and picnicking.

11. The Alaskan Aviation Museum celebrates the state's aviation history. Located at the Anchorage International Airport, the museum features the Hall of Fame, exhibits, tours, and more.

12. Alaska Botanical Garden showcases the state's native plants and northern horticulture. Located in Anchorage, you'll find 1,100 species of perennials and more than 100 plants that are native to Alaska. If regional horticulture interests you, this is one attraction you won't want to miss.

13. Denali has temperature extremes, which can reach -75 degrees Fahrenheit with wind chills of -118 degrees Fahrenheit. It has been said that these temperatures can cause a person to freeze within seconds.

14. Chena Hot Springs is a popular attraction in Fairbanks, Alaska. The hot springs are in the middle of a 40 square mile geothermal area. With temperatures reaching 165 degrees Fahrenheit, the stream of water needs to cool down before people can soak in it. Today, it's privately owned. You can visit the Chena Hot Springs Resort to enjoy the springs.

15. The Aurora Ice Hotel used to be a hotel that was made entirely of ice. It made for a pretty unique overnight experience for tourists. However, the hotel was shut down because it lacked smoke detectors. Yeah, you read that right.

16. The Alaska Wildlife Conservation Center, which is located in Portage Valley, is dedicated to

preserving the state's wildlife. Some of the animals you can expect to find include reindeer, wolves, black bears, Grizzly bears, foxes, and bison.

17. Lake Clark National Park is a 4,030,015-acre park that attracts approximately 20,000 visitors each year. Lake Clark, which spans 50 miles, is a popular place to go kayaking.

18. The Juneau Icefield is the fifth largest icefield in North America. The icefield is believed to have caused several glaciers in the region, including Mendenhall Glacier.

19. Sitka National Historical Park is rich in Alaskan history. It preserves the site of a battle that took place between the native Kiks.ádi Tlingit and Russians. You'll find a totem pole, as well as the restored house that belonged to the Russian Bishop. If you're a history buff, this is one Alaskan attraction you won't want to miss out on.

20. The largest active sand dunes in the Arctic can be found in Kobuk Valley National Park.

Test Yourself – Questions and Answers

1. The largest national park in the country, which can be found in Alaska, is:

    a. Denali National Park
    b. Glacier Bay National Park
    c. Wrangell-St. Elias National Park

2. Alaska's No. 1 tourist attraction is which of the following?

    a. Portage Glacier
    b. Denali National Park
    c. The Alaska Zoo

3. The name of the Alaska Zoo's first animal was:

    a. Annabelle
    b. Maggie
    c. Jezebel

4. The most climbed mountain in Alaska is:

    a. Denali
    b. Flattop Mountain
    c. Mount Hunter

5. Alaska's national park, which is the least visited national park in all of America, is:

    a. Wrangell-St. Elias National Park
    b. Kobuk Valley National Park
    c. Gates of the Arctic National Park

Answers

1. c.
2. b.
3. a.
4. b.
5. c.

CHAPTER FIVE

ALASKA'S INVENTIONS, IDEAS, AND MORE!

Inventions, foods, and ideas have come out of every state. Have you ever wondered what originated from Alaska? Although there are many inventions which have grown popular throughout the entire country, some remain indigenous to Alaska's culture and tourism. Here are some of the most popular things that have come from Alaska!

Hidden Valley Ranch Dressing

Today, it's a condiment staple in America, but did you know that ranch dressing originated from Alaska?

It all started out back in 1949 when Nebraskan plumber Steve Henson and his wife, Gayle, moved to Alaska. Steve worked as a plumbing contractor in the remote Alaskan bush. He cooked in order to feed his crew and came up with a salad dressing concoction to encourage them to enjoy the salads he was serving them. He mixed up the ingredients he had on hand: mayonnaise, buttermilk, and some herbs and spices. The salad dressing turned out to be a hit.

After working in Alaska for three years, Henson and his wife moved to California in 1954. They bought the Sweetwater Ranch, a dude ranch, which they renamed Hidden Valley. They served Steve's dressing on the dude ranch, where it began to grow popular. The Henson's began to charge 75 cents for envelopes of powdered ranch dressing mix throughout the entire country.

In 1973, Steve Henson sold his brand and production for $8 million. Today, Hidden Valley Ranch dressing can be found on any grocery store shelf.

The Electric Razor

Did you know the inspiration for the electric razor came from Alaska?

When retired U.S. Army Lieutenant Colonel Jacob Schick (yes, of the Schick razor brand) went gold mining in Alaska, he came up with the idea of the electric razor.

In order to shave in Alaska, you had to collect ice and melt it. When he was collecting ice, Schick sprained his ankle—which led him to want to come up with something more convenient and less dangerous than collecting ice.

Schick built his own motor, and ten years later, in 1933, he applied for a patent for the electric razor.

By 1937, Schick's razor had had almost two million sales.

Reindeer Dogs

If you're visiting Alaska and you have a hankering for a hot dog, you're probably going to come across a "Reindeer Dog."

These hot dogs are made from—you guessed it—reindeer, otherwise known as caribou. They're made by two companies: Indian Valley Meats, which makes a hot dog that's a mix of beef and reindeer with natural casing, and Alaska Sausage and Seafood, which sells smoked reindeer links, seasoned with coriander. They're traditionally served with Coca-Cola grilled onions, mustard, and/or cream cheese.

Wondering what Reindeer Dogs taste like? They've been compared to venison sausage, only with a less gamey flavor.

This street food, which is popular in Anchorage, has begun to spread across the country. Biker Jim has a cart that sells them in Denver, Colorado. Who knows? You might even find Reindeer Dogs in your hometown soon.

Kayaks

Did you know the kayak originated from Alaska? They date back to 4,000 years ago when the Inuit made kayaks to hunt on the rivers, lakes, and coastal waters.

The kayaks that are used today are quite very modern compared to the kayaks of those times. The Inuit made their kayaks from a frame made of either wood or whale bones. The region the Inuit lived in determined what their frames were made of. The Inuit living in the west used wood, since trees were available in the area, while the Inuit of the east used whalebones.

The Inuit would then cover their kayaks with animal skins. The animal skins they used to cover their kayaks came from walrus, seals, sea lions or caribou. They treated the animal skins with oil every four to eight days to keep them waterproof.

The size of the Inuit kayaks was approximately 17 feet long by less than 2 feet wide and 7 inches deep.

Although the Aleut, Yupik, and possibly the Ainu also made kayaks for hunting, the Inuit are credited with the invention.

The word "kayak" is also derived from the Inuit language. The word "kayak" comes from the Inuit word "qayaq," which has a translation of "man's boat" or "hunter's boat." The word "kayak" is believed to have entered the European language because Dutch or Danish whales encountered the Intuit while they were hunting whales in Greenland.

Powdered Beer

If you're a beer connoisseur, you might have a hard time believing powdered beer is really a thing, but it is.

Powdered beer was invented by Pat's Backcountry Beverages. The beer powder comes in a pouch, which will make a 16 oz. beer when added to water. The powder is made from sodium bicarbonate and citric acid. It also comes with a carbonated plastic bottle that turns flat beer into a fizzy, more beer-like substance.

The product is currently waiting for a patent.

Will powdered beer be the next invention with SodaStream or Keurig fame? It's believed that this could be a revolutionary invention for the beer industry, but time will tell.

Eskimo Ice Cream

Have you ever heard of Eskimo Ice Cream?

The Yupik call it "akutaq," which means "something mixed." What ingredients are mixed to make this food? Well, its ingredients just may surprise you. It's not what most Americans think of when they think of ice cream." In fact, it's not really ice cream at all.

Traditionally, Eskimo Ice Cream is made from wild berries (such as cranberries, salmonberries, crowberries, and/or blueberries), fish, tundra greens, roots, and animal oil or fat. Seal oil is typically used, as well as fat and/or meat from reindeer, moose, walrus, and/or whitefish. Snow might be added, which is called "snow akutaq."

In the more modern versions of Eskimo Ice Cream, ingredients like sugar, milk, and Crisco are added.

It's unlikely that you'll find this food outside of Alaska, but who knows?

Birch Syrup

Maple syrup is an American breakfast staple, but did you know there's also a thing called birch syrup? Although no one knows for sure where it was invented, Kahiltna Birchworks in Alaska is a popular company that produces it.

Derived from the sap of birch trees, Alaska birch syrup has a different flavor from maple syrup. It also can be eaten on more than just pancakes. Since it has a lower sugar content than maple syrup, birch syrup is commonly used in desserts, salad dressings, and fish glazes.

The flavor has been compared to a citrusy honey.

Looking for more reason to try it? It's considered to be one of the rarest gourmet food products in the *entire world*, as it's one of the most difficult foods to produce. It takes about 100 to 150 liters of birch sap to produce just one liter of syrup, which is double the amount of sap it takes to produce maple syrup.

Poop Scoop

Have you ever wondered who to thank for the invention of the dog Poop Scoop?

A dog kennel owner named Richard Martin of Chugiak, Alaska invented the product. He designed his Poop Scoop out of an antifreeze jug and a long pole with something that worked like a rake. When it worked successfully for six years, he knew it was a keeper. Martin had the product patented in 2003.

Poop Moose Candy Dispenser

You've probably seen it during the holidays or as a gag gift: a wooden moose that you fill with M&Ms. When you lift the moose's head, the M&Ms get dispensed from its butt.

The product was designed by Darryl Fenton of Wasilla, Alaska. The product, as seen on *QVC*, had sold more than 100,000 by 2003.

Although the craze has died down, you can still buy the Poop Moose Candy Dispenser.

Snowshoes

It may come as no surprise to learn that some of the first snowshoes in the United States were designed by the Inuit.

The Inuit had two different snowshoe styles, one which was triangular in shape and about 18 inches long, and one that was circular in shape.

What might surprise you, though, is that the Inuit rarely used their snowshoes. During the winter, the majority of their travels were done by walking on ice or the tundra. The snow wasn't too deep in these areas, eliminating the need for snowshoes.

Ulu Knives

You may already know by now that ulu knives were invented by the Alaskan natives more than 3,000 years ago. They invented the knives when the Europeans taught them how to use metal.

The traditional ulu knife's handle was made from walrus ivory, caribou antler, or muskox horn. Sometimes, wood or bone was used to make the handle.

Ulu knives were traditionally used by the Inuit, Yupik, and Aleut women during those times. The knives served a number of purposes, the most common of which were skinning and cleaning animals, cutting food, and cutting hair. Ulu knives were, at times, used as weapons. Sometimes,the natives also s used them to trim blocks of ice and snow when they were building igloos.

In modern times, the handles of ulu knives are generally made with caribou antlers or a hardwood. The blade of the knife is typically made of steel, which is derived from hand or wood saws. Ulu knives continue to be used by Alaska's natives, and they are commonly sold at souvenir shops throughout the state.

Mukluks

Mukluks are a soft boot that's traditionally made from the hide of reindeer or seals. Did you know they were designed by the Inuit, Yupik, and Inupiat natives of Alaska?

The word "mukluk" originated from the Inupiat and Yupik word "maklak," meaning "bearded seal."

Today, the word mukluk is frequently used to describe any soft cold weather boots that are made from animal skin, including UGG boots.

Parkas

Did you know that parkas originated from Alaska? They were invented by the Caribou Inuit of Canada. The origins of the first parka in America can be traced back to Alaska's natives.

A parka is a coat that has a fur-lined hood. Traditionally, the first parkas were made using seal or caribou skin. They were worn when the natives when hunting and kayaking in the harsh weather conditions. The coats were typically treated with oil in order to remain waterproof.

Sunglasses

Did you know the Inuit and Yupik have been credited with inventing the world's first sunglasses?

Okay, so, *technically*, they were snow goggles, but their purpose was to prevent snow blindness. They designed to block a person's eyes from the brightness, allowing light to only enter in two small slits that were cut out for visibility.

Traditionally constructed of whale bone, driftwood walrus ivory, and/or caribou antler, the goggles were carved to tightly fit the person's face. The idea was to fit the goggles tight enough so that the only light that could enter was through the slits. Soot was sometimes added on the inside of the goggles to help reduce the glare.

Baked Alaska

Baked Alaska didn't actually come from Alaska. That being said, Baked Alaska—as the dessert's name might lead you to guess—was inspired by Alaska.

There are several stories about where exactly Baked Alaska originated from. The most commonly accepted claim was that the dessert recipe was invented by a chef named Charles Ranhofer, who worked at Delmonico's restaurant in New York in 1867. Ranhofer came up with the dessert in celebration of the United States purchasing Alaska from Russia.

The dessert consisted of cake, a layer of ice cream, and browned meringue. Although the dessert recipe was originally going to be called Alaska-Florida as a way to describe its cold and hot layers, the cake ended up being called Baked Alaska instead.

RANDOM FACTS

1. Muktuk is a native Alaskan specialty. If you like sushi, this one might be for you. It's a combination of frozen whale skin and blubber, which is eaten raw.

2. Fried wild halibut and chips is a popular dish in Alaskan cuisine.

3. Reindeer sausage is a popular dish in Alaska. People eat it with their breakfast, in a "Philly" sandwich, or by itself.

4. While sourdough bread was *not* invented in Alaska, it did gain some traction in the state. Sourdough bread was actually first brought to California from France. When Californians headed to Alaska during the Klondike Gold Rush, they brought sourdough bread with them. Since yeast and baking powder weren't readily available in Alaska, gold miners would carry backpacks full of starters to make their own sourdough bread. It was so frequent in the region that the term "sourdough" was applied to people who protected their starters and old-timers. The term is still frequently used to describe any Alaskan or Klondike old-timer today.

5. Denali Dreams Soap Co. is a company that sells natural soaps. The company colors their soaps with herbs, spices, and natural pigments and uses essential oils for scents. The soaps are a hit among tourists.

6. The most versatile warcraft of all-time was invented in Alaska.

7. Alaska Glacial Mud's skincare products are made from the state's glaciers. The company's facial masks and mineral soaps are made from glacial mud derived from the Copper River.

8. Yak burgers can be found on most Alaskan restaurant menus.

9. The Eskimo yo-yo is a toy that generally has two leather balls on each end that are fur-covered, connected by a twine. The toy is played by the Inupiat and Yupik. It's a popular toy among Alaskans and is often found in souvenir shops throughout the state.

10. Wild halibut tacos and fajitas are a popular food among Alaskans.

11. Salmon salsa is a unique form of salsa, full of both salmon and peppery seasoning. The company that makes them, Salsa Salmon, is based in Anchorage.

12. In addition to Reindeer Dogs, Indian Valley Meats sells jerky, pepper sticks, trail salsa, and more!

13. Smoked salmon chowder is Alaska's version of clam chowder. Full of smoked salmon, the creamy chowder is a favorite among Alaskans. Gwin's Lodge in Cooper Landing on the Kenai Peninsula is a popular spot for the fare.

14. The Alaskan Brewing, Co. offers a number of beers with themed names, including "Hopothermia" and "Icy Bay IPA."

15. Reindeer steaks are a popular entrée in the state.

16. Echo Lake Meats is well-known for its Jalapeno Cheese Spread and offers an array of other products, including Double Smoked Game Hens, Alaskan Smoked Salmon Spread, specialty sausages, and more.

17. Kenai Premier BBQ Sauce is a company on the Kenai Peninsula that offers an array of BBQ sauces that range from Mild to Extra Spicy. The company has recently begun to expand, with retail outlets opening in Oregon and other states.

18. Yummy Chummy dog treats are made in Alaska. They're made from Alaska salmon and come in a variety of flavors.

19. Tonka Seafoods is the largest sockeye salmon processing country in all of Alaska.

20. King crab is a popular fare among both Alaskans and tourists of the state.

Test Yourself – Questions and Answers

1. Which salad dressing was invented in Alaska?

   a. Italian dressing
   b. Blue cheese dressing
   c. Ranch dressing

2. Which Alaskan invention was *not* created by the natives?

   a. Mukluks
   b. Parkas
   c. Powdered beer

3. The word "kayak" comes from the word "qayaq," meaning "man's boat" or "hunter's boat." Which Alaskan native language does "qayaq" come from?

   a. Aleut
   b. Inuit
   c. Yupik

4. Californians who traveled to Alaska during the Klondike Gold Rush brought what invention with them?

   a. Sourdough bread
   b. Rain boots
   c. Snow Tires

5. Which toy was popular among Alaska's natives?

    a. The Hula Hoop

    b. The Eskimo Yo-Yo

    c. The Eskimo Tire Swing

Answers

1. c.
2. c.
3. b.
4. a.
5. b.

CHAPTER SIX

ALASKA'S BIGGEST HAUNTS, SUPERNATURAL, AND OTHER WEIRD FACTS

Have you ever wondered what urban legends exist in Alaska? Have you ever considered what creepy legends or unsolved mysteries haunt the state? There are a number of urban legends about Alaska, mainly thanks to Inuit and Alaskan native mythology. The cold ocean and many remote geographic areas in Alaska also play a big role in its folklore.

But this chapter goes beyond urban legends and myths that are common in the state. Have you heard about the largest mass killing that happened in the state? Do you know about the serial killer who once made his kills in Alaska? Or about one of the most controversial (and eerie) government programs that were based in the state?

What you learn in this chapter may creep you out. It might give you goosebumps. It might even leave you feeling haunted. If you're ready for that, then read on!

The Qalupalik is Said to Snatch Children

The Alaskan natives have a Bigfoot of their own. It's called the Qalupalik, a legendary creature that originated from the Inuit. In the Inuit language, the meaning of the word Qalupalik is "monster."

The Qalupalik is said to look like a mix between a humanoid and monster. It's believed to have green skin, long hair, and long fingernails. The monster, which is believed to be female, is said to carry an amautik, which is a type of parka that Inuit women use to carry their children in. It's the monster's intentions that have scared the Inuit the most, however.

The Qalupalik is said to hum to lure children to her. If the children wander too far away from their families and too close to the seashore, she puts them in her amautik and takes them back to the sea with her. In most versions of the tale, she raises the children as her own. In others, she drags them to their death.

The Inuit people have long told this story to their children to get them to behave. It helped prevent their children from wandering off or going too close to the water.

Alaska's Largest Mass Murder Remains

Unsolved

The largest Alaskan mass murder of all time has yet to be solved.

It happened back in September of 1982 when the *Investor*, a fishing boat, had gone up in flames in Craig, Alaska. There were eight passengers inside, who had all been shot with a .22-caliber gun.

The victims in the mass murder were 28-year-old Mark Coulthurst and his pregnant wife, their two children, and four of the ship's crew members. They were murdered just hours after celebrating Mark's birthday.

The details of the case are quite disturbing, but the biggest question is who committed this heinous crime?

A man, who was believed to be in his 20s, was thought to be responsible for the murders. Here's what the authorities claim happened: after he murdered his victims, the man drove the boat to a secluded bay and waved to the passengers of a nearby vessel, who didn't suspect anything. Dropping off the boat in the bay, the man left the boat and went back to the docks. He came back the following day, this time with a can of gasoline. He set the *Investor* on fire, sped back to town, and disappeared.

One suspect named John Peel was arrested for the crime, based on similarities in his appearance and sketches of the suspect. Peel had previously worked for Coulthurst. It was suggested that they'd had a falling out. Peel was working on another ship at the time of the crime.

The case, which was built upon circumstantial evidence, went to trial twice. The first trial resulted in a hung jury, and the second trial ended with Peel being found not guilty of the crime. Former police detective David McNeill, who helped with the investigation, still believes Peel is the one who committed the crime and that they let the wrong guy go free.

But what if McNeill is wrong? What if Peel really *didn't* do this mass murder spree? Then who did?

That's the question everyone in Craig wants the answer to.

Another theory that has been bounced around is that the *Investor* was a drug ship. Craig, Alaska was said to have been a hotspot for drugs at the time. Adding fuel to that theory was the fact that the *Investor*, a ship which had cost more than $800,000, was the most expensive ship in the area at the time.

Recognized as "Alaska's worst unsolved mass homicide," the case has been closed. Even so, the mass murder continues to haunt the town's locals.

Not only do people wonder *who* committed the crime, but they also wonder *why*, as no motive has ever been proven.

The Monster That's Said to Haunt Iliamna Lake

You've heard of the Lochness Monster, but have you heard of the Iliamna Lake Monster?

It has long been said that there's something lurking around the waters of Iliamna Lake. In fact, the Tlingits allegedly named the lake after a mythical great blackfish that was said to bite holes in the kayaks of "bad" natives.

The Tlingits also spoke of a Gonakadet, a legendary wolf-headed orca. The Aleuts saw what they called a "Jig-ik-ak" monster fish, which they believed traveled in groups and killed people who were traveling by boat.

While none of these things seem to have existed, there's believed to be something just as creepy lurking in the waters of Iliamna Lake. There have allegedly been sightings of a large, white creature that is said to resemble the Lochness Monster. The monster is believed to be 10 to 30 feet in length with a square head. There have been reports of the monster using its head to deliver blunt force to small boats.

The most well-known sighting of the monster happened back in 1967 when a guy named Chuck

Carpuchettes was flying over the lake in his plane and happened to spot the monster. He and his friend later decided to fish for the monster. They went out on a float plane and baited their hooks with caribou. Something in the water not only bit one of the hooks, but it also towed the plane around the lake with it. While the meat had disappeared, nothing was ever caught that day.

There have been a number of theories of what the monster might be. Some believe that it could be Pacific sleeper sharks that are able to live through the winter thanks to pockets on the bottom of the lake. There was a video shared on YouTube back in 2012, which depicted a smaller Pacific sleep shark in the Iliamna Lake.

Others believe that it could be a white sturgeon, which has somehow managed to survive in Lake Iliamna since the Ice Age. Jeremy Wade of the *Animal Planet* TV show *River Monsters* is a believer in this theory.

Maybe someday we'll find out what's really lurking in Lake Iliamna. Until then, we'll just have to wonder what's hiding out in the lake.

Alaska's Most Controversial Government Program

Did you know that one of the most controversial (and downright creepy) government programs of all-time was based in a facility that performed its operations in Alaska?

High Frequency Active Auroral Research Program, otherwise known as HAARP, was a government-based research program that began in 1990. Most of its funding came from the U.S. Navy, the U.S. Air Force, and the University of Alaska. Late Senator Ted Stevens helped secure the program's funding. The program's purpose was to analyze the ionosphere, a portion of the upper atmosphere that's affected by the sun.

Seems reasonable enough, right? Well… maybe. But maybe not. The program has drawn a lot of conspiracy theorists, who believe it was actually designed to control the weather… and maybe even more than just the weather.

Back in 2010, Venezuelan leader Huge Chavez made claims that HAARP, or a similar program, was behind the Haiti earthquake. According to him, weather control caused the earthquake to occur.

Some conspiracy theorists believe that HAARP *did*, in fact, cause this and other natural disasters—and a whole lot more. They believe the program could control the weather, was responsible for global warming and even participated in mind control.

Of course, conspiracy theories are sometimes just that: conspiracy theories. But things get weirder. In his book, *Angels Don't Play This HAARP*, Nick Begich, Jr. (son of the late U.S. Representative Nick Begich) says that some of these claims are true. In fact, he actually says that HAARP was able to trigger earthquakes and more. Begich also claims on his website that HAARP was a mind control device.

The thing is, Nick Begich, Jr. isn't alone in questioning HAARP or its true motives.

Former Minnesota Governor Jesse Ventura questioned the facility's intentions. Ventura requested to visit the facility, but he was turned down. Now, why would a government research program deny a governor the right to visit?

What's more is that Bernard Eastlund, a physicist, has said that HAARP's technology was developed from his own patents—patents that he claims have the ability to change the weather and satellites.

The Alaska state legislature has even held hearings about the facility due to environmental concerns.

To make things weirder (if you can even *get* any weirder at this point), the HAARP program permanently shut down in 2014.

So, what was really going on there? The world may never know.

Bigfoot is Frequently Sighted in Alaska

Bigfoot is one of America's biggest legends. Just about every state has had reports of alleged sightings of Sasquatch-like creatures, but did you know that Bigfoot is said to run rampant through the Last Frontier?

The thing is, it makes a lot of sense that Bigfoot would call Alaska home. With its thick forests, remoteness, low population, and uncharted territories, there's no doubt that the state would make a great hideout for Bigfoot.

The Bigfoot Field Researchers Organization says there have been 21 reported Bigfoot sightings in the state, with eight of those taking place in or near Fairbanks. The island of Prince of Wales is also said to be a Bigfoot sighting hotspot, with a mayor even calling in the crew of the Animal Planet's *Finding Bigfoot*.

When an earthquake that took place near Kodiak Island in January of 2018, Alaskan Natives reportedly saw Bigfoot-like creatures heading up the hillside to get to higher grounds.

Bigfoot sightings have been so common that it drew the attention of the *Animal Planet* show, *Finding Bigfoot*. The mayor of Hydaburg, Alaska asked the crew to investigate some suspicious footprints. While they were there, the crew came across what may have been a Bigfoot footprint. They also talked to a woman who allegedly had a log thrown at her taxi and spotted what may have been Bigfoot in a tree.

But perhaps the creepiest Bigfoot story of all comes from Port Chatham, which is located on the Kenai Peninsula. During the 1900s, mangled bodies kept washing ashore in the small village. People were so convinced that evil Sasquatch spirits were behind the deaths that they eventually all abandoned the village out of fear.

The Alaska Bushman is One of Alaska's Most Popular Legends

The Alaska Bushman is one of the most well-known legends from the state. The Alaska Bushmen, or Tornit, is said to be a race of very large people, which were once said to exist throughout the United States and Alaska.

Stories of the Alaska Bushman go back to when the Inuit and Tornits once peacefully coexisted in nearby villages. At one point, they even shared common hunting grounds. So, what happened to change this peaceful coexistence?

While the Inuit people frequently built kayaks for hunting, the Alaskan Bushmen allegedly didn't know how to build one. And this is where the two groups allegedly ran into problems.

The story goes like this: a young Tornit borrowed a kayak that belonged to a young Inuit without permission and damaged the bottom of the boat. Feeling angry and revengeful, the young Inuit killed the Tornit in his sleep. Afraid that they would be next, the other Tornits fled from the country.

Since then, there have been stories of hunters disappearing. Were the Tornit responsible for the killings? Or is it merely a coincidence that some hunters were allegedly found dead, while others were never seen again?

A lot of people have even questioned if the Tornit could be Bigfoot.

The Legend of the Adlet

The legend of the Adlet is… well, beyond silly, to say the least. That being said, it's one of the most well-known urban legends to come out of the state. Like so many of Alaska's myths, the legend of the Adlet traces back to Inuit folklore.

The Adlet is believed to be a race of people that are half-human, half-dog. They aren't believed to resemble a werewolf, however. Whereas werewolves can assume the form of wolf *or* human, the Adlet is believed to resemble both human and dog. It's said that their upper bodies are human, while their lower half is dog, similar to that of a centaur (which is half-human, half-horse).

141

Okay, so here's where things start to get really unbelievable. Folklore says that the Adlet are the result of an Inuit woman mating with a dog. The woman is said to have given birth to 10 children, five of which were Adlet and the rest of which were dogs. The family got sent away to a remote island, but their grandfather continued to hunt for food for them from the mainland. The Inuit woman's dog husband swam from the island to the mainland every day. There, the grandfather would wrap a pair of boots filled with meat around the dog's neck. One day, however, the grandfather filled the boots with rocks. The dog husband drowned. The Inuit woman feared for her children's lives. She sent them inland, where they continued to produce more Adlet.

Today, the Adlet are believed to be aggressive savages who will attack any man who they cross paths with.

The strangest part about it all? There's a version of the story that also exists in Greenland, where the "Adlet" are instead known as the "Erqigdlit." Researchers have linked the Greenland version of the tale to the werewolf.

The Reason So Many People Go Missing in Alaska is a Mystery

Did you know that Alaska is notorious for missing persons? In fact, it's been estimated that approximately five out of every 1,000 people going missing in Alaska. This is more than double the national average as far as missing persons go. The question is: why?

With the state's forests, remote locations, and harsh weather conditions that reach below freezing temperatures, there's no doubt that it's easy to go missing. Many believe that the cause of so many disappearances in Alaska goes beyond that, however.

You've probably heard of the Bermuda Triangle, but have you ever heard of the "Alaska Bermuda Triangle" or the "Alaskan Triangle"? It has been theorized that Alaska could contain a space vortex, due to the large number of magnetic anomalies that can be found in the state. The vortex is believed to be able to transport things into another dimension, which could potentially explain why so many people—and objects—go missing in the state every year.

The Alaskan Triangle is believed to be spread across a large portion of the state. If it exists, it apparently ranges from the southeastern region near Juneau to Anchorage, in the middle of the state, to the Barrow Mountain range in northern Alaska. A lot of the area is unexplored and uncharted—and it's a common place for people to go missing.

It's been estimated that 16,000 people have disappeared in this region since 1988. Not only have tourists and Alaska state residents gone missing, never to be heard from again, but a number of planes have also disappeared without a trace. Planes have also crashed in the area, seemingly without cause. Despite rescue efforts by state troops, these people are rarely found... dead or alive.

In 1950, a military craft that was carrying more than 40 passengers disappeared. No wreckage was ever found. It may have been just a little creepy, but then it kept happening; more planes continued to go missing without a trace.

One noteworthy plane that went missing belonged to House Majority Leader, Hale Boggs, back in 1972. Boggs' plane went missing somewhere between Anchorage and Juneau. The search efforts were *huge*, with 50 civilian planes and 40 military aircraft participating in the search efforts. For more than a month, 32,000 square miles were searched, but no wreckage or remains were ever found.

Of course, the Alaskan Triangle isn't the only theory out there that explains these disappearances. Remember the Kushtaka, who lure children away from their families? If you ask the Inuit, that's the real reason people tend to go missing without a trace in the state.

The Tizheruk May Be Lurking in Alaskan Waters

The Tizheruk are large, snake-like sea creatures that are believed to occupy Alaska's waters. As if Alaska needs something else in its waters that you need to fear, right?

The Tizheruk, which are said to reside near Key Island, AK, is thought to be approximately 12 to 15 feet long. They allegedly have a 7-foot long head and a tail with a flipper. If you wish to avoid them, you could try staying away from the water, but that might not even help.

If you plan to spend any time on Alaska's docks or piers, watch out! According to local lore, the Tizheruk would snatch people from docks and piers without people even noticing they were there.

Alaska is Known for UFO Sightings

Did you know that UFOs are frequently reported in the Last Frontier? As of 2018, Casino.org listed Alaska as one of the top 10 states with the most reported UFO sightings.

Some conspiracy theorists believe that Alaska is a popular place for UFOs due to the state's low population and its significant amount of remote land.

In 2018, reports of UFO sightings increased after an

earthquake. Is it possible that extraterrestrial beings—or whoever is flying the unidentified flying objects—were trying to get away from the natural disaster?

Mount Hayes, which is the highest mountain in eastern Alaska, is believed to be a hotspot for UFOs and possibly aliens. Sightings in the area began back in the 1940s. The reports of sightings were so frequent that the FBI even began to investigate the region.

Military personnel reported strange incidents over the course of the next 50+ years. In the late 1990s, a former CIA by the name of Pat Price said the mountain was home to the largest number of aliens in the country.

One creepy incident involving UFOs took place back in 1986. A Japanese plane that was traveling to Anchorage from Iceland came across three UFOs. The UFOs followed the airliner above the Alaskan wilderness, and even through the Alaska Triangle. One of the UFOs was described as double the size of an aircraft carrier. It was believed to be some sort of mothership. The pilots made extreme efforts to try to avoid the UFOs, but the eerie objects continued their pursuit of the airliner for almost 400 miles. When the plane got close to Fairbanks, the UFOs finally backed off. Creepy much?

Alaska Once Had a Serial Killer

Did you know that there was once a serial killer in the state of Alaska?

Robert Hansen, who was referred to as the "Butcher Baker" in the media, did his killing spree in Anchorage. He was responsible for kidnapping, raping, and murdering at least 17 women between 1971 and 1983. It's believed that he may have killed up to 30 women during that time period.

What you're about to read next may disturb you.

Hansen owned a private plane. After he held the women captive and raped them for long periods of time, he would then fly them to a remote area. Hansen would then release the women into the wild and hunt them like animals, using a Ruger Mini-14 Ranch Rifle and a knife to kill them.

Robert Hansen only ended up being caught because one of his victims escaped in 1983 and let the police know what was happening.

Hansen was sentenced with 461 years, a life sentence, and no possibility of parole.

The 2013 movie *The Frozen Ground*, which features John Cusack and Nicholas Cage, was based on the case.

The Keelut May Follow You

Another one of Alaska's most popular legends is the Keelut. The Keelut is said to be an evil earth spirit, which takes the form of a dog that only has hair on its feet.

The Keelut are believed to follow people who are traveling at night before attacking and killing them.

How do you know if one is nearby? Well, if you see a dog tracks that suddenly disappear, you can expect that the Keelut must be in the region.

With all of the wild dogs in the state (wolves, foxes, coyotes, and sled dogs), it's hard to say how you'd really know if a Keelut was following you.

Alaska's Haunted Ghost Town

Have you ever wondered what the most haunted spot in Alaska is?

An old abandoned copper mine located outside of McCarthy, Alaska, is said to be the most haunted spot in the Last Frontier.

The Kennecott Copper Mine was once an extremely active mine. It produced thousands of jobs and gave the town of McCarthy a huge economic boom for about 30 years.

Sadly, the railroad that ran through the area stopped being used because of the high cost associated with changing its position, thanks to a glacier in the area. The mine suddenly become a ghost town—a ghost town that's really said to be haunted. In fact, it's even been called the most haunted spot in all of Alaska.

Some of the paranormal activity that people have reported in the area is pretty creepy. For example, people have claimed to see tombstones appear and then disappear on the hiking trails in the area. There have also been reports of children crying and poltergeist activity.

In the 1990s, state government workers were in the area to create a housing project development. However, they were driven away due to paranormal activity in the area. The ghosts even allegedly began to steal the workers' tools from their belts and tool boxes.

Unless you're a ghost hunter, this is one ghost town you might want to steer clear of.

Alaska's Haunted Russian Castle

The United States' purchase of Alaska took place at Russia's Baranof Castle, which is located in Sitka, Alaska. Today it's known as Castle Hill in Sitka. It's a popular tourist attraction that's said to be haunted by a woman who wears blue or black.

The supposed haunting of the castle goes way back. Before the Alaska Purchase took place, there were stories of the ghost of a mourning lady who wears dark clothing. The ghost was said to belong to that of a Russian aristocrat, who was being forced to marry a man she wasn't in love with and committed suicide on the night of the wedding.

The King Bear's Skull May Have Been Found

An unusually large, elongated polar bear skull was found in 2014, which may have belonged to a "king bear." King bears are commonly discussed in Inuit mythology. Also known as "weasel bears," the Inuit claimed that king bears were an enormous polar bear with a narrow body that "moved as fast as a demon."

The skull, which experts claim is vastly different from polar bears of modern times, may give some credibility to this myth. The bear skull was estimated to be from 670 to 800 AD.

RANDOM FACTS

1. The northern lights are a source of many different theories. The Tlingit and Kwakiutl believed the aurora borealis was caused by human spirits dancing. The Inuit believed that the spirits were playing a ball game, during which they used a walrus skull as the ball. Some of the natives also believed that the colors of the aurora borealis were actually the spirits of dancing animals—deer, salmon, seals, and beluga, especially. Another common myth about the northern lights? Conceiving a child beneath the northern lights will lead that child to have a very lucky life.

2. The Motherlode Lodge in Palmer, Alaska is said to be one of the state's most haunted hotels. There have been reports of figures being sighted in mirrors, a black cloud-like apparition that wanders the grounds, and strange noises that have been heard in the middle of the night. Some guests have even reported their curtains being mysteriously opened.

3. With its remote location, the never completed Igloo City Hotel is widely regarded as one of the state's creepiest places. There have also been

reports of a woman in white seen in the windows of the old abandoned hotel. She allegedly flicks lights on and off.

4. The Kushtaka are said to be shape-shifters that resemble the cross between an otter and a man. Although some people have claimed the Kushtaka are friendly creatures, most believe they're a form of a siren. They allegedly mimic the screams of women and children to lure male fisherman in order to steal their souls. Although this could easily be passed off as just a myth, there have been alleged counters with the Kushtaka in the 1900s. The Thomas Bay area of Alaska is where the majority of these encounters have taken place. Back in the 1900s, a gold prospector said he was chased by an entire pack of Kushtaka. The gold prospector talked about his encounter, not caring how insane anyone thought it sounded, and then never returned to the area ever again.

5. The Captain Cook Hotel is one of the most popular hotels in Anchorage, and it's also said to be one of the most haunted. A woman once committed suicide at the hotel. Her ghost is believed to haunt the women's restroom. Guests have also claimed that doors open and close on their own and lights mysteriously flick on and off.

6. The Alaska Museum of Aviation is said to be haunted. Staff members have reportedly seen the ghosts of a man and a woman. Mysterious and unexplainable voices and footsteps have also been heard.

7. The Headless Valley Monster is said to be a wolf-like evil spirit in the Nahanni Valley. Inuit folklore says that the monster kills people by biting off their heads. Although the monster is believed to primarily live in the Headless Valley in Canada, there have been sightings in Alaska as well. An American mechanic who believes he saw the monster described it as a "wolf on steroids." The crew of the TV show *Alaska Monsters* claimed they almost had an encounter with the creature. Cryptozoologists have theorized that the Headless Valley Monster may actually be a saber wolf, which is thought to be descendant of the Dire Wolf that lived during the Ice Age. No one knows for sure if saber wolves exist, but some believe they may live in small populations in Alaska.

8. Fishermen have reported seeing the Kodiak Island Sea Monster over the years. The monster is said to have a long neck, a horse-like head, and nostrils that act as blowholes. Unlike most water monsters, it's said to live in the sea, not in a lake. There have been reported sightings as recently as

2002. Since it lives in the ocean, experts think it's likely that the Kodiak Island Sea Monster could have been a species that has survived since the prehistoric times.

9. A University of Alaska Anchorage student named Bonnie Craig never showed up for class one day. Later that day, her body was found floating in McHugh Creek. Severe head injuries indicated that Craig had fallen off a cliff. While Alaska State Troopers believed she had been injured while hiking, Bonnie's mom suspected that her daughter was murdered. Her mom believed Bonnie's undercover work with the police department may have had something to do with her death. An informant told the Craig family that Bonnie may have been targeted by a drug lord, whose arrest she had been involved in. To this day, her death, which was featured on *Unsolved Mysteries*, has yet to be resolved.

10. There's rumored to be a ghost who haunts Anchorage's West High School. There have been reports of the female ghost, who is said to haunt the auditorium, for decades. People have claimed to see her standing silently among the seats when the auditorium is dark, exiting through corridors, and hanging out backstage or in the basement hallways. People have also reported strange paranormal activity, such as unexplained doors

slamming, lights flickering, and the sound of footsteps in empty hallways. The stories of the ghost have always been consistent. She's always wearing white. Students also aren't the only ones who have claimed to see the West High School Ghost. School officials and visitors have also seen her, and many had never even heard about a ghost prior to their own reports.

11. The Tariaksuq might be the eeriest of all the Inuit legends. These humanoid creatures are believed to be similar to humans. They live in houses, have families, and do other ordinary human things. The difference is that Tariaksuq isn't visible when you look at them directly. This causes them to disappear into another world that they live in. When they are killed, the Tariaksuq become fully visible to anyone who looks at them. In some versions of the tale, they can also appear half-human, half-caribou.

12. Each Alaskan native tribe had its own thoughts on the raven, but many of Alaska's natives believed that the raven isn't to be trusted. Regarded as a trickster, the raven is believed to be a shapeshifter who can take the form of any human or animal. The raven is believed to be unpredictable by nature and a keeper of secrets. Most also believed that the raven was a gluttonous bird who was willing to sacrifice anything to satisfy its own

desires. The Haida tribe, however, believed that ravens were heroic. They believed that the raven discovered the world's first humans hiding in a clamshell and that the bird brought them salmon and berries to survive. The Tlingit tribe, on the other hand, believed that there were two types of ravens. They believed in the selfish, gluttonous, sneaky raven, but they also believed that the other raven was responsible for bringing light to darkness, as well as for creating the world.

13. The Inuit believed in Ijiraq, a word which translates to "shapeshifter." They are believed to be unpredictable and complex monsters since they can appear in any form they wish. The Ijiraq kidnap children, who they hide and abandon. If the children are able to convince the Ijiraq to let them go, the Inuksugaq (a stone landmark) will help guide them home. This is another one of those tales that the Inuit used to help their children behave better.

14. The remains of an unidentified sea creature were discovered by a kayaker near Juneau. He thought it was a type of ray at first, but he quickly realized that it was something much larger. Experts said they believed it could be the liver of a Pacific sleeper shark, but the size of the object would have meant the sleeper shark was far larger than any in existence. It's also unclear how

the liver may have become separated from a sleeper shark's body. So, what was it really? The world may never know.

15. The Alaskan natives told stories of a bird called the "thunderbird." The bird, which is said to be enormous, was believed to hunt by throwing giant snakes the natives referred to as "lightning snakes" at whales and other marine animals that it preyed on. In 2002, however, there were reports of a bird that was said to be the size of a small plane. The bird was reportedly said to be something you'd see in a *Jurassic Park* movie.

16. The legend of the Ocean Spider originated from the Inuit, who claim there's a monster that lurks in the depths of shallow waters. The monster allegedly preys on kayakers. When a kayaker gets too close to the monstrous spider, it jumps out at them and eats them.

17. The Historic Anchorage Hotel is one of the most popular places in the city to stay, as well as one of the most haunted. The city's first chief of police was killed near the hotel. People have claimed to have spooky encounters with a spirit that's believed to be him. Guests have also reported seeing the spirit of a woman dressed in white who roams the hotel's halls, along with ghost children.

18. Hundreds of mummies have been found on the Aleutian Islands. Despite the harsh weather conditions, the mummies were preserved similarly to the Egyptian mummies.

19. The Akhlut is a dangerous beast that originated from Inuit legends. It was believed to be the spirit of an orca that would shapeshift into a wolf or that would resemble a half-orca, half-wolf when it was out of the water. You'll know if one is nearby because its tracks lead to and from the sea. Inuit believed dogs coming to or from the ocean were evil.

20. The Inuit believed the Qiqirn to be a bald dog spirit. Although people are afraid of it is, it is afraid of people as well. The Qiqirn is said to only have hair on its feet, mouth, and the tip of its tail. Shouting its name can scare it away. In *The Second Jungle Book*, Rudyard Kipling wrote a short story about the Inuit and the Qiqirn called "Quiquern."

Test Yourself – Questions and Answers

1. Jeremy Wade of the show *River Monsters* believes the Iliamna Lake Monster is actually a _____.
   a. Sleeper Shark
   b. Lochness Monster
   c. White Sturgeon

2. Which mountain is believed to be a hotspot for UFOs?
   a. Mount Hayes
   b. Denali
   c. Flattop Mountain

3. Alaskan natives believed the Northern lights were actually:
   a. Dancing spirits
   b. Evil spirits
   c. Balls of fire

4. How many people go missing in Alaska every year?
   a. 1 out of 5,000
   b. 5 out of 5,000
   c. 500 out of 5,000

5. Which Inuit legend was the result of a human woman reproducing with a dog?
   a. The Adlet
   b. The Qualipak
   c. The Tariaksuq

Answers

1. c.
2. a.
3. b.
4. b.
5. a.

DON'T FORGET YOUR FREE BOOKS

GET THEM FOR FREE ON
WWW.TRIVIABILL.COM

OTHER BOOKS IN THIS SERIES

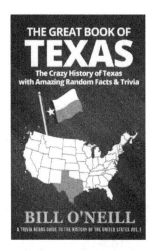

Are you looking to learn more about Texas? Sure, you've heard about the Alamo and JFK's assassination in history class, but there's so much about the Lone Star State that even natives don't know about. In this trivia book, you'll journey through Texas's history, pop culture, sports, folklore, and so much more!

In The Great Book of Texas, some of the things you will learn include:

Which Texas hero isn't even from Texas?

Why is Texas called the Lone Star State?

Which hotel in Austin is one of the most haunted

hotels in the United States?

Where was Bonnie and Clyde's hideout located?

Which Tejano musician is buried in Corpus Christi?

What unsolved mysteries happened in the state?

Which Texas-born celebrity was voted "Most Handsome" in high school?

Which popular TV show star just opened a brewery in Austin?

You'll find out the answers to these questions and many other facts. Some of them will be fun, some of them will creepy, and some of them will be sad, but all of them will be fascinating! This book is jampacked with everything you could have ever wondered about Texas.

Whether you consider yourself a Texas pro or you know absolutely nothing about the state, you'll learn something new as you discover more about the state's past, present, and future. Find out about things that weren't mentioned in your history book. In fact, you might even be able to impress your history teacher with your newfound knowledge once you've finished reading! So, what are you waiting for? Dive in now to learn all there is to know about the Lone Star State!

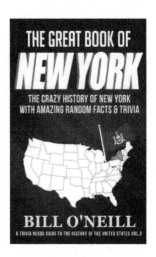

Want to learn more about New York? Sure, you've heard about the Statue of Liberty, but how much do you really know about the Empire State? Do you know why it's even called the Empire State? There's so much about New York that even state natives don't know. In this trivia book, you'll learn more about New York's history, pop culture, folklore, sports, and so much more!

In The Great Book of New York, you'll learn the answers to the following questions:

- Why is New York City called the Big Apple?
- What genre of music started out in New York City?
- Which late actress's life is celebrated at a festival held in her hometown every year?
- Which monster might be living in a lake in New York?

- Was there really a Staten Island bogeyman?
- Which movie is loosely based on New York in the 1800s?
- Which cult favorite cake recipe got its start in New York?
- Why do the New York Yankees have pinstripe uniforms?

These are just a few of the many facts you'll find in this book. Some of them will be fun, some of them will be sad, and some of them will be so chilling they'll give you goosebumps, but all of them will be fascinating! This book is full of everything you've ever wondered about New York.

It doesn't matter if you consider yourself a New York state expert or if you know nothing about the Empire State. You're bound to learn something new as you journey through each chapter. You'll be able to impress your friends on your next trivia night!

So, what are you waiting for? Dive in now so you can learn all there is to know about New York!

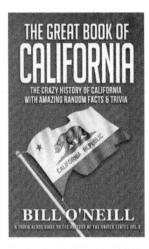

Are you interested in learning more about California? Sure, you've heard of Hollywood, but how much do you really know about the Golden State? Do you know how it got its nickname or what it was nicknamed first? There's so much to know about California that even people born in the state don't know it all. In this trivia book, you'll learn more about California's history, pop culture, folklore, sports, and so much more!

In The Great Book of California, you'll discover the answers to the following questions

- Why is California called the Golden State?
- What music genres started out in California?
- Which celebrity sex icon's death remains a mystery?
- Which serial killer once murdered in the state?
- Which childhood toy started out in California?

- Which famous fast-food chain opened its first location in the Golden State?
- Which famous athletes are from California?

These are just a few of the many facts you'll find in this book. Some of them will be entertaining, some of them will be tragic, and some of them may haunt you, but all of them will be interesting! This book is full of everything you've ever wondered about California and then some!

Whether you consider yourself a California state expert or you know nothing about the Golden State, you're bound to learn something new in each chapter. You'll be able to impress your college history professor or your friends during your next trivia night!

What are you waiting for? Get started to learn all there is to know about California!

MORE BOOKS BY BILL O'NEILL

I hope you enjoyed this book and learned something new. Please feel free to check out some of my previous books on <u>Amazon.</u>

Made in the USA
Monee, IL
18 June 2023

36104863R00105